CATHOLIC VALUES IN THE
AUSTRALIAN PUBLIC SQUARE

CATHOLIC VALUES IN THE AUSTRALIAN PUBLIC SQUARE

Joseph Santamaria

Connor Court Publishing
Ballarat

Published in 2014 by Connor Court Publishing Pty Ltd

PO Box 224W
Ballarat VIC 3350
sales@connorcourt.com
www.connorcourt.com

ISBN: 9781925138030 (pbk.)

Cover design by M. Giordano

Printed in Australia

CONTENTS

Overview

This publication is essentially a collection of essays that were written independently of each other to serve as commentaries on a variety of issues.

Section I is devoted to a problem that has slowly emerged in the field of science which is becoming corrupted by a combination of ideological factors and vested interests of individuals and institutions. Over a period of 30 years, these developments have engaged the attention of political activists and involved legislative measures as well as the distribution of large sums of money to scientific organisations.

To illustrate this phenomenon, I have gathered several documents from my archives which were written in response to specific events that impacted on my specialties of community medicine and bioethics. The first essay I have entitled "The Pope and the AIDS Experts" which I wrote in 2009 but was not published as I set it aside for further development. This essay opened up another related field in medicine that became known as the era of "Evidence-based Medicine". At that time, in the 1980s and 1990s, a major activity of the Department of Community Medicine at St. Vincent's Hospital in Melbourne was the Alcoholism Clinic, later expanded into the field of Drug Abuse. To the second essay I have given the title "Drug Abuse and Evidence-based Medicine".

Section I continues with a commentary on an interesting initiative by the World Health Organization and its Reproductive

Health Library and use of the Cochrane Review System. This is followed by commentaries on the "Effectiveness of condoms in the AIDS epidemic and the role of the mainstream media".

Section 2 is devoted to the question of Politics and Religion. The first essay was written in 2004 when national elections were held in Australia and the United States of America. A vigorous debate occurred in both countries over the issue of religious values being imposed on a secular society. The first essay is called simply "National Elections and Religious Values". The second is titled "The Family and the Political System". It was an after dinner speech that I gave to a mainly Catholic organisation in 2010. Concluding this section is the essay "Reason and Faith in the New Millennium". It was written in 2007 and was based on addresses given by Pope Benedict XVI during the previous year.

Section 3 has three articles that are loosely related. They are written from my own perspective as a practising Catholic layman and enter the field of Christian theology. As a personal hobby, I have privately studied in the fields of philosophy, theology and bioethics, but have no academic degrees in these fields except insofar as I wrote them for journals of several voluntary organisations. The first paper is a spiritual reflection on the Eucharist (2005), "I am the Way, the Truth and the Life". The second is entitled "Musings on the Godhead". This was written as an hypothesis in February this year (2013) as I tried to combine my knowledge in science, theology and philosophy. Finally the last essay is self-explanatory – "A Mixed Up Catholic Layman". I wrote it for the publisher of this book, Anthony Cappello, who shows many of the same symptoms. I thank him for his interest and valuable advice.

Dedication

This collection of unpublished essays has been assembled in order to dedicate the resulting book to the recently retired Pope Benedict XVI. The essays have been written over the last 10 years but their subject matter remains in the public square where passionate debate continues. Benedict XVI has been a central figure in all these issues where he has manifested great courage, profound learning, exemplary teaching skills and a deep commitment to the Catholic faith and the commission given by Christ to His Apostles and their successors.

I have quoted freely from other sources in order to clarify the issues that have generated opposing responses and to open up the available documents that need to be read. Many of these responses were articulated by Benedict XVI but in the ensuing debates, some of his comments were distorted or misinterpreted. My own participation was somewhat peripheral as these essays were mainly given as speaking engagements for a variety of organisations.

I can appreciate the problems that confronted Benedict XVI in recent years. Advancing age is a natural phenomenon and so too are the physical and cognitive disabilities that arise along the way. A schedule that makes extraordinary physical and mental demands is too exhausting for an elderly individual; the range of activities he was expected to perform exceeded his physical competence.

Benedict XVI has made a courageous decision to surrender the Papacy at this stage in the history of the Catholic Church. I have long admired his intellect, his capacity to listen to friend and foe alike, his humility and his dignity and the depth of his devotion to the Lord Jesus Christ. His legacy is profound but his greatest attribute has been his witness as the Vicar of Christ on this earth.

Doctor Joseph Santamaria
August 2013

SECTION ONE

The Corruption of Science

Preamble

The first section of this publication is a set of related essays that deal with evidence-based medicine as it has evolved in the last twenty years and was starkly highlighted by Pope Benedict XVI's trip to Africa in March 2009. It uses the technique of analysing the statements made by some authors by first quoting in full their commentaries as they appeared in published form. I have done it this way to bring out the fact that there is considerable scientific support for the words of the Pope, but that there is an ideological suppression of this evidence by pejorative attacks on those who raise their voices in support of a change in current promiscuous sexual behaviour in sub-Saharan Africa.

What changed the public debate on climate change was access to basic data and original sources of knowledge that had been either suppressed by vested interests or misinterpreted or twisted by some members of the scientific community or bureaucrats. It was aided and abetted by the advent of the modern computer which has enormous power to crunch numbers. This enabled statisticians to formulate models of climate changes by their manipulation of the data, their "cherry-picking" and by the weighting of the various selected variables. This in turn led to their claim of a "scientific consensus" and their attack on the deniers (aka sceptics). Their "scientific consensus" was in fact a consensus of the leaders of some scientific institutions that are precariously dependent on massive government funding and of an amorphous group of business entrepreneurs and others seeking power through political channels.

Today, the word "consensus" has become a very contentious expression, especially when it is implicitly assumed to be synonymous with accepted fact. The fact is that scientific truth, just like any truth about ultimate reality, is not determined by a consensus of scientists, politicians or lobbyists but by established facts and the robustness and rigour of all the available evidence.

The second section deals with problems that today confront Christianity and the Catholic Church in particular. It is a time when the churches are striving to converse with a "pandemic" of secular forces that are intolerant of religious values and see no point in a dialogue between science, politics and religion.

Pope Benedict XVI had taken the bold step of re-evangelisation and insisting on the use of reason and factual evidence to support his messages. It is an opportune time to do so when science is losing its credibility by inserting ideology as a basic premise for the selection and analysis of scientific data, and using computer predictive modelling to justify dangerous political decisions across a range of disciplines, such as environmental science, economics, statistical analyses, history and biology, etc.

The use of the internet together with other technological devices have transformed the speed and range of distribution of news and opinions throughout the world; communication has become global and virtually instantaneous. A side development of this phenomenon is the tendency of journalists, newspaper editors, radio commentators and television presenters to "sensationalise" the news, which often distorts the truth and bypasses proper verification and analysis of contentious issues.

These are some of the matters that I deal with in this publication of musings over the last 30 years. In reviewing my archives of past essays that I have written, I am astonished how relevant and passionate they remain in the public square of debate in the year 2013.

In using this technique of quoting liberally from original sources, I have often inserted my own comments. My personal commentaries have the suffix (JNS).

1
The Pope and the AIDS experts

On his way to Africa for a pastoral visit to the Cameroons and Angola in 2009, Pope Benedict XVI was asked: "Holy Father, among the many evils that affect Africa, there is also the particular problem of the spread of AIDS. The position of the Catholic Church for fighting this evil is frequently considered unrealistic and ineffective."

The question was asked by a journalist in the press corps that accompanied the Pope on the flight to the Cameroons. We do not know whether the journalist was aware of the role of the Catholic Church in the care of the victims of the AIDS epidemic on the African continent, or whether he was just preoccupied with the distribution and use of condoms in the prevention of AIDS or the use of supervised injection programmes among intravenous drug users.

The issues to be considered are so complex and the vested interests of so many people in this field of medicine and human behaviour are so diverse, that no-one could give a detailed response without a meticulously prepared document.

What the Pope said
The Pope responded by saying quite succinctly:

I would say the opposite. I think that the reality that is most effective, the most present and the strongest in the fight against AIDS, is precisely that of the Catholic Church, with its programmes and its diversity. I think of the Sant'Egidio Community, which does so much visibly and invisibly in the fight against AIDS … And of all the sisters at the service of the sick.

I would say that one cannot overcome this problem of AIDS only with money – which is important, but if there is no soul, no people who know how to use it, (money) doesn't help.

One cannot overcome the problem with the distribution of condoms. On the contrary, they increase the problem. The solution can only be a double one: first, a humanisation of sexuality, that is, a spiritual human renewal that brings with it a new way of behaving with one another; second, a true friendship even and especially with those who suffer, and a willingness to make personal sacrifices and to be with the suffering. And these are factors that help and that result in real and visible progress.

Therefore I would say this is our double strength – to renew the human being from the inside, to give him spiritual human strength for proper behaviour regarding one's own body and toward the other person, and the capacity to suffer with the suffering … I think this is the proper response and the Church is doing this, and so it offers a great and important contribution. I thank all those who are doing this.

Commentary (JNS)

What the Pope is saying here is that the Catholic Church is offering Africa a multi-pronged service in the management of the AIDS epidemic in Africa. There is plenty of evidence of the range of services that the Catholic Church provides in Africa and worldwide. It is a very impressive contribution to the victims of this epidemic.

He is also implying that the free handouts of condoms in the prevention of the disease in Africa is misguided for the fundamental problem is widespread promiscuous sexual behaviour in a culture that has other contributing factors to the spread of this infection. Casual, uncommitted sexual behaviour with a multitude of scattered sexual partners and a resultant expansion in the prevalence of the disease makes "catching" the disease almost inevitable over time for this promiscuous heterosexual population.

This is what the scientific evidence reveals as reported by a world authority on AIDS and by health workers in the field.

Edward C. Green, director of the AIDS Prevention Research Project at the Harvard Center for Population and Development Studies, has said that the evidence confirms that the Pope is correct in his assessment that condom distribution exacerbates the problem of AIDS.

"The Pope is correct," Green told *National Review Online* on 18 March 2009, "or to put it a better way, the best evidence we have supports the Pope's comments. He stresses that "condoms have been proven to not be effective at the "level of population." Green adds: "There is a consistent association shown by our best studies, including the US funded 'Demographic Health Surveys', between greater availability and use of condoms and higher (not lower)

HIV-infection rates. This may be due in part to a phenomenon known as risk compensation, meaning that when one uses a risk-reduction 'technology' such as condoms, one often loses the benefit (reduction in risk) by 'compensating' or taking greater chances than one would take without the risk-reduction technology."

Green continues: "I also noticed that the Pope said 'monogamy' was the best single answer to African AIDS, rather than 'abstinence.' The best and latest empirical evidence indeed shows that reduction in multiple and concurrent sexual partners is the most important single behaviour change associated with reduction in HIV-infection rates (the other major factor is male circumcision)."

That comment from a research scientist, specialising in the field of the AIDS epidemic worldwide, attracted an instant reprisal from the AIDS brotherhood.

An editorial appeared in the English medical journal *The Lancet* (Vol. 373, Issue 9669, p. 1054, 28 March 2009). The following is the full text.

Redemption for the Pope?

The Vatican felt the heat from an unprecedented amount of international condemnation last week after Pope Benedict XVI made an outrageous and wildly inaccurate statement about HIV/AIDS. On his first visit to Africa, the Pope told journalists that the continent's fight against the disease is a problem that "cannot be overcome by the distribution of condoms: on the contrary, they increase it".

The Catholic Church's ethical opposition to birth control and support of marital fidelity and abstinence in HIV prevention is well known. But, by saying that condoms exacerbate the problem of HIV/AIDS, the Pope has publicly distorted scientific evidence to promote Catholic doctrine on this issue.

The international community was quick to condemn the comment. The governments of Germany, France and Belgium released statements criticising the Pope's views. Julio Montaner, president of the International AIDS Society, called the comment "irresponsible and dangerous". The United Nations Programme on HIV/AIDS (UNAIDS), the UN Population Fund, and (World Health Organization (WHO) released an updated position statement on HIV prevention and condoms, which said that "the male latex condom is the single, most efficient, available technology to reduce the sexual transmission of HIV". Amidst the fury, even the Vatican tried to alter the pontiff's wording. On the Holy See's website, the Vatican's head of media, Father Federico Lombardi, quoted the Pope as having said that there was a "risk that condoms … might increase the problem".

Whether the Pope's error was due to ignorance or a deliberate attempt to manipulate science to support Catholic ideology is unclear. But the comment still stands and the Vatican's attempts to tweak the Pope's words, further tampering with the truth, is not the way forward. When any influential person, be it a religious or political leader, makes a false scientific statement that could be devastating to the health of millions of people, they should retract or correct the public record. Anything less from Pope Benedict XVI would be an immense disservice to the public and health advocates, including many thousands of Catholics, who work tirelessly to try and prevent the spread of HIV/AIDS worldwide.

Commentary (JNS)

Could all those prestigious bodies quoted in the editorial not be strictly right or maybe even wrong? Did the Pope's reported statements constitute "a deliberate attempt to manipulate science to support Catholic ideology"? From what does the Pope have to be redeemed? Does Edward Green have to be redeemed from his intervention?

Virtually all of the vitriolic attacks made by the media, the scientific community and secularist commentators are rhetorical statements, all premised on the belief that the "scientific evidence" is incontrovertible. But none gives a bibliography of their sources. None talk about their methodology in the field, except for Green. Some suggest that there is no evidence to support the claim that condoms promote promiscuity without giving any evidence that scientific studies have positively proven their own claims.

This is what Green had to say after the passionate furor of the "experts" had spent itself (*The Washington Post*, 29 March 2009).

The Pope May Be Right

When Pope Benedict XVI commented this month that condom distribution isn't helping, and may be worsening, the spread of HIV/AIDS in Africa, he set off a firestorm of protest. Most non-Catholic commentary has been highly critical of the Pope. A cartoon in the *Philadelphia Inquirer*, reprinted in *The Post*, showed the Pope somewhat ghoulishly praising a throng of sick and dying Africans: "Blessed are the sick, for they have not used condoms."

Yet, in truth, current empirical evidence supports him.

We liberals who work in the fields of global HIV/AIDS and family planning take terrible professional risks if we side with the Pope on a divisive topic such as this. The condom has become a symbol of freedom and – along with contraception – female emancipation, so those who question condom orthodoxy are accused of being against these causes. My comments are only about the question of condoms working to stem the spread of AIDS in Africa's generalised epidemics – nowhere else.

In 2003, Norman Hearst and Sanny Chen of the University of California conducted a condom effectiveness study for the United Nations' AIDS programme and found no evidence of condoms working as a primary HIV-prevention measure in Africa. UNAIDS quietly disowned the study. (The authors eventually managed to publish their findings in the quarterly *Studies in Family Planning*.) Since then, major articles in other peer-reviewed journals such as *The Lancet*, *Science* and *BMJ* have confirmed that condoms have not worked as a primary intervention in the population-wide epidemics of Africa. In a 2008 article in *Science* called "Reassessing HIV Prevention" 10 AIDS experts concluded that "consistent condom use has not reached a sufficiently high level, even after many years of widespread and often aggressive promotion, to produce a measurable slowing of new infections in the generalised epidemics of Sub-Saharan Africa."

Let me quickly add that condom promotion has worked in countries such as Thailand and Cambodia, where most HIV is transmitted through commercial sex and where it has been possible to enforce a 100 per cent condom use policy in brothels (but not outside of them). In theory, condom promotions ought to work everywhere. And intuitively, some condom use ought to be better than no use. But that's not what the research in Africa shows.

Why not?

One reason is "risk compensation". That is, when people think they're made safe by using condoms at least some of the time, they actually engage in riskier sex.

Another factor is that people seldom use condoms in steady relationships because doing so would imply a lack of trust. (And if condom use rates go up, it's possible we are seeing an increase of casual or commercial sex.) However, it's those ongoing relationships that drive Africa's worst epidemics. In these, most HIV infections are found in general populations, not in high-risk groups such as sex workers, gay men or persons who inject drugs. And in significant proportions of African populations, people have two or more regular sex partners who overlap in time. In Botswana, which has one of the world's highest HIV rates, 43 per cent of men and 17 per cent of women surveyed had two or more regular sex partners in the previous year.

These ongoing multiple concurrent sex partnerships resemble a giant, invisible web of relationships through which HIV/AIDS spreads. A study in Malawi showed that even though the average number of sexual partners was only slightly over two, fully two-thirds of this population was interconnected through such networks of overlapping, ongoing relationships.

So what has worked in Africa? Strategies that break up these multiple and concurrent sexual networks – or, in plain language, faithful mutual monogamy or at least reduction in numbers of partners, especially concurrent ones. "Closed" or faithful polygamy can work as well.

In Uganda's early, largely home-grown AIDS programme, which began in 1986, the focus was on "Sticking to One Partner" or "Zero Grazing" (which meant remaining faithful within a polygamous marriage) and "Loving Faithfully". These simple messages worked. More recently, the two countries with the highest HIV infection rates, Swaziland and Botswana, have both launched campaigns that discourage people from having multiple and concurrent sexual partners.

Don't misunderstand me; I am not anti-condom. All people should have full access to condoms, and condoms should always be a backup strategy for those who will not or cannot remain in a mutually faithful relationship. This was a key point in a 2004 "consensus statement" published and endorsed by some 150 global AIDS experts, including representatives of the United Nations, WHO and World Bank. These experts also affirmed that for sexually active adults, the first priority should be to promote mutual fidelity. Moreover, liberals and conservatives agree that condoms cannot address challenges that remain critical in Africa such as cross-generational sex, gender inequality and an end to domestic violence, rape and sexual coercion. Surely it's time to start providing more evidence-based AIDS prevention in Africa.

A powerful article was written by Deidre Fleming in Western Australia. She is currently (2009) conducting research at the John Curtin School of Medical Research in Canberra.

It appeared in *The Record*, the weekly newspaper of the Catholic Archdiocese in Perth.

AIDS & the Pope

"Blind faith trumping common sense," "Vatican insiders declare the Pope a disaster," "Outrageous," "Irresponsible," … If anything is embarrassing, it is the sensationalism of such statements in the Western media when giving the party line of anti-Catholic sentiment. The trouble is that when one looks at the science of AIDS research today, one finds a completely different story from the one being promoted by the popular media.

Whose expert opinion?

The problem for the layman is that certain organisations which sound authoritative make claims which are regarded as "expert opinions".

For example, the International AIDS Society has denounced Pope Benedict XVI's comments as "contrary to scientific evidence and global consensus" and has suggested that his comments might even exacerbate HIV infection in Africa.

In the same vein, the president of the World Health Assembly, Leslie Ramsammy, has claimed, "The statement by the Pope is inconsistent with science, it's inconsistent with our experiences and it is not in sync with what Catholics have experienced and believe," while Kevin Osborne of the International Planned Parenthood Federation says, "All the evidence is that preaching sexual abstinence and fidelity will not solve the problems ... The Pope's message will alienate everybody. It is scary. It spreads stigma and creates a fertile breeding ground for the spread of HIV."

On the other hand, authorities in the field who disagree with these sorts of statements get scant media attention. Here I am not talking about renegade scientists, but professionals in HIV/AIDS research who provide technical reports to the WHO and UNAIDS.

Take, for example, Edward Green, director of Harvard University's AIDS Prevention Research Project (APRP): in an interview with CNA, Green stated with reference to Africa, "Theoretically, condoms ought to work, and theoretically, some condom use ought to be better than no condom use, but that's theoretically ... We just cannot find an association between more condom use and lower HIV infection rates."

This view is echoed by Helen Epstein, specialist in public

health in developing countries and consultant to Human Rights Watch. In a 2008 letter to UNAIDS she bemoans the disconnect between on-the-ground research about condoms and UN reports: "I seem to recall UNAIDS documents attributing the decline in HIV infections in US gay men to the rise of 'the condom culture'. In fact, modeling studies by Martina Morris and behavioural surveys carried out across the US show that partner reduction was dramatic during the 1980s, when HIV decline among gays was the steepest. The "condom culture" emerged only later. I can provide many references on this, on request." She goes on to say, "Condom use alone may have protected many individuals, but has not – in the absence of partner reduction – shown a strong epidemiological effect, anywhere. One may not like this fact, but it is true."

Condoms, though seemingly an effective technological fix, have had their greatest influence in AIDS prevention when targeted towards such areas as the sex industry in Thailand.

But even then, the UNAIDS best practice reports fail to mention that there was a 60 per cent decline in visits to brothels during Thailand's condom campaign and that this undoubtedly contributed to the decline in HIV.

Why are condoms so ineffective?

The trouble with condoms is that they have the effect of giving users a false sense of security which results in disinhibition, that is, users indulge in greater risk taking which eventually negates any protective effects of the condom.

According to Potts et al, "When most transmission occurs within more regular and, typically, concurrent partnerships, consistent condom use is exceedingly difficult to maintain."

James Shelton of the Bureau for Global Health, USAID, in Washington DC puts it this way: "Many people dislike using them (especially in regular relationships), protection is imperfect, use is often irregular, and condoms seem to foster disinhibition, in which people engage in risky sex either with condoms or with the intention of using condoms."

"Condom use with prostitutes and in one-night stands is increasingly the norm all over the world, but they are rarely used in longer-term, less businesslike affairs," observes Helen Epstein.

Know your epidemic

It is becoming increasingly clear to AIDS researchers that some of the assumptions that underlie HIV prevention strategies are unsupported by the evidence.

Some of the confusion is created by a failure to differentiate adequately between different types of epidemics. Outside of Africa (in Europe, the Americas, Middle East, Asia and Australasia) HIV tends to occur among high risk groups: men who have sex with men, injecting drug users, sex workers and their partners.

These are known as concentrated epidemics. Africa, particularly Southern and Eastern Africa, on the other hand, is an example of a generalised epidemic, with infection predominantly heterosexual and generalised among the population.

Then there are epidemics such as those in the Caribbean, Pacific region, the horn of Africa and West Africa which may include characteristics of both concentrated and generalised epidemics.

According to James Shelton ten myths impede the success of AIDS prevention in Africa. These misconceptions include beliefs such as that poverty and conflict increase vulnerability to HIV and that transmission occurs through sex workers and promiscuous men or adolescents; whereas current research seems to indicate that most transmission occurs because of the prevalence of multiple and simultaneous or concurrent partnerships among adults in African society.

Helen Epstein describes it this way in her article, "The Fidelity Fix": "This 'concurrency' links sexually active people up in a giant network, not only to one another but also to the partners of their partners' partners – and to the partners of those partners, and so on – via a web of sexual relationships that can extend across huge regions. If one member contracts HIV, then everyone else in the web may, too." Helen Epstein and Daniel Halperin of Harvard's Centre for Population and Development Studies explain it this way: "In Africa, many longer term relationships that do not involve prostitution nevertheless tend to have a powerful 'transactional' element. People with more disposable income might thus be able to maintain multiple, concurrent relationships. Although very few are 'rich' by Western standards, they are nevertheless at the leading edge of the massive social and economic transition occurring in Africa today, from an agrarian past to a semi-industrialised present, characterised by rapid urbanisation, high unemployment, and lack of social security. As with all such transitions, this creates upheavals in basic norms, customs and values, which might facilitate the spread of HIV."

In an opinion piece for *The Lancet*, James Shelton states, "Our priority must be on the key driver of generalised epidemics – concurrent partnerships … But partner limitation (fidelity) has also been neglected because of the culture wars between advocates of condoms and advocates of abstinence, because it smacks of moralising, because mass behavioural change is alien to most medical professionals, and because of the competing priorities of HIV programmes.

David Wilson of World Bank and Daniel Halperin of the Harvard School of Public Health agree:

"For too long, the global HIV-prevention community has pursued generalised responses in concentrated epidemics, concentrated approaches in generalised epidemics, or hedged their bets and done a bit of everything," they said in *The Lancet* in August 2008.

"For example, after three decades, the global community is only beginning to accept that there is no simple direct association between income, education, gender inequality, and HIV. Population-based surveys show that the wealthier

African countries have the highest, not the lowest, infection levels in Africa, and more educated, upper-income people are generally more likely to be infected with HIV."

They say that it is "striking that a comparison of gender equality and HIV prevalence across African countries shows a strong positive, not negative, association." That is, wherever women and men are most equal, HIV is most prevalent. Contrast Botswana, the second wealthiest country in Africa, with rare male circumcision, high levels of multiple concurrent partnerships and an HIV prevalence of 25 per cent, with Niger, the lowest ranking country in the Human Development Index, predominantly Muslim with strict sexual constraints and universal male circumcision, but an HIV prevalence of 0.7 per cent.

"Turning to generalised epidemics," continue Wilson and Halperin, "we face three overarching challenges. First, our most trusted prevention interventions – testing and counselling, condom promotion, school and youth programmes, and treatment of other sexually transmitted infections … are at best unproven, and at worst disproven, for reducing HIV incidence. Second, the most solidly proven preventive intervention to date, male circumcision, is barely advancing … In countries such as Zambia, with 15 per cent adult HIV prevalence and nearly US$ 1billion in aid annually for AIDS, much less than one per cent of this funding goes for male circumcision services … Third, the major contributor to reduced HIV transmission in generalised epidemics has been reduction in multiple sexual partnerships (increased fidelity). Compelling evidence of this association has emerged in a growing number of African countries, such as Kenya, Zimbabwe and Ethiopia. Additionally, partner reduction seems to have contributed to HIV declines in Haiti and the Dominican Republic. Yet, except for Uganda in the late 1980s, and more recently in Swaziland, reductions in multiple partnerships seem to have mainly occurred despite, not because of, formal programmes."

What happened in Uganda?

In 1993, Helen Epstein was working as a molecular biologist in Uganda, at that time the country with the highest HIV-infection rate in the world. She explains how HIV incidence plummeted from 21 per cent in 1991 to six per cent in 2002.

"At the time, few international health experts were working on AIDS in Uganda, but the Ugandan government developed a simple and effective programme on its own. In 1986, the Uganda Ministry of Health started a vigorous HIV-prevention campaign in which the slogans "Love Carefully", "Love Faithfully" and "Zero Grazing" – Ugandan slang for "Don't have sexual partners outside the home" – were posted on public buildings, broadcast on radio and bellowed in speeches by government officials, teachers and AIDS-prevention workers across the country.

"Religious leaders scoured the Bible and the Koran for quotations about infidelity. Newspapers, theatres, singing groups and ordinary people spread the same message. Their words fell on fertile ground ... A realistic fear of

AIDS was reinforced by a compassionate response to the suffering the disease created. Ordinary Ugandans have always been much more open about AIDS than people from other African countries, and they were also far more likely to admit that they knew someone who had died of the disease or was infected with HIV. Community – and church-based groups sprang up to help families affected by AIDS. Uganda's women's movement, one of the oldest and most dynamic in Africa, galvanised around issues of domestic abuse, rape and HIV.

"The anger of the activists, and the eloquent sorrow of women throughout the country who nursed the sick and helped neighbours cope, was a harsh reproach to promiscuous men. So was their gossip, a highly efficient method of spreading any public-health message."

An article by Potts et al in *Science* explains it as follows: "In Uganda, HIV prevalence declined dramatically following the extensive 'Zero Grazing' campaign of the late 1980s. WHO surveys conducted in 1989 and 1995 found a greater than 50 per cent reduction in the number of people reporting multiple and casual partners. In Kenya, partner reduction and fidelity also appear to have been the main behavioural change associated with the recent HIV decline.

"Similar behaviour change has been reported in DHS surveys in Zimbabwe, where HIV has also fallen, along with Ethiopia, Côte d'Ivoire, and urban Malawi. In Swaziland, the number of people reporting two or more partners in the past month was halved after an aggressive 2006 campaign focusing on the danger of having a 'secret lover'."

Reassessing the funding

Potts and his team plead for a reassessment of funding for interventions that have the greatest potential impact.

In a letter responding to comments by the Department of Evidence, Monitoring and Policy at UNAIDS, they say, "We note that the requested funding for [hyper-endemic and generalised] epidemics would comprise only a little over 20 per cent of the global total, even though such epidemics account for over two-thirds of all HIV infections worldwide."

"Also, although 5 per cent of this funding would be dedicated to circumcision programmes, the large majority of resources would continue to be allocated to other interventions, for which the evidence of prevention impact in generalised epidemics is much weaker ... Recent CDC data from Uganda suggest that most married people who recently acquired HIV were infected by an extramarital partner or by their spouse who had recently acquired HIV from an extramarital partner. Many of the latter were probably in the brief "acute infection" period, when HIV infectivity is much higher yet undetectable by a standard HIV test. It is crucial to address the multiple and concurrent partnerships that mainly drive these generalised epidemics." A growing number of AIDS experts who are prepared to look at the facts are questioning why the Ugandan approach has not been emphasised in Southern Africa and elsewhere.

Edward Green in his book *Rethinking AIDS Prevention* says,

"There is also a troubling suspicion among a growing number of scientists who support the ABC model that certain opponents may simply be AIDS profiteers, more interested in protecting their incomes than battling the disease."

His book, *AIDS and Ideology*, due for release later this year, highlights the AIDS funding industry which is "drawing billions of dollars a year promoting condoms, testing, drugs and treatment of AIDS".

Claiming that AIDS has been spread because of the lack of human rights for "vulnerable populations", such as homosexual men and sex workers, the UN, in the document *International Guidelines on HIV/AIDS and Human Rights*, have suggested that AIDS cannot be defeated unless all international laws restricting human sexuality are amended:

"Criminal law prohibiting sexual acts (including adultery, sodomy, fornication and commercial sexual encounters) between consenting adults in private should be reviewed, with the aim of repeal."

The *Guidelines* also promote abortion on demand, legalisation of homosexual marriage, and laws "providing penalties for vilification of people who engage in same-sex relationships".

It seems that to the UN, AIDS funding is more about promoting the ideologies of the sexual revolution than about using the research to promote public health.

"To treat one AIDS patient with life-prolonging anti-retroviral drugs costs more than US$1,000 a year. Our successful ABC campaign cost just 29 cents per person each year," explains Sam Ruteikara, co-chair of Uganda's AIDS Prevention Committee.

David Kalema, Ugandan AIDS activist, puts it poignantly in the film *The Change is On*, which documents the Catholic Church's approach to behaviour modification in South Africa and Uganda:

"Maybe they tried [abstinence] and it failed, and since it failed with them, they think it will fail with everyone. I'm a testimony myself. I finished my primary [school] without having sex. I went for my secondary education, I didn't have sex, I went to University, I was not having sex. I never fell sick because of not having sex. Can this world tell me that it only worked with me? The way it worked with me it can work with everyone else. My friends who used to laugh at me thinking that abstinence is abnormal, most of them are dead by now."

Deirdre Fleming is a former Science Educator, and is currently undertaking Postgraduate Studies in Public Health at Curtin University.

Commentary (JNS)

An Interesting article was written by Dr. James Shelton, a Global Health Research Officer, which appeared in *The Lancet* in December 2006. Using the language of scientific studies in AIDS research documents, he said exactly what the Pope, two years later, claimed about the catastrophe of the AIDS epidemic in Africa.

The media and some scientists in the AIDS establishments promptly descended like a flock of scorched eagles on the Pope, blaming the Catholic Church for the hyper-epidemic of the disease in sub-Saharan Africa, by its condemnation of the use of condoms based not on science but on dogmatic religious belief. But the scientists did not act in that way with Shelton. They just tried to ignore him or avoided publishing his commentaries or by claiming that his analysis was faulty.

Some historical evidence

Some historical evidence is enlightening. Early in the epidemic in the Western world, it was noted that certain populations of people were prone to get the disease. The first was the male homosexual community, traced by the Centers of Disease Control in the USA. The second was the population of people who had received contaminated blood or blood products. The third was intravenous drug users. The fourth was so-called sex workers and their clients. And finally there was the phenomenon of spread in the African continent.

In other words, there were different populations (what the epidemiologists call "heterogeneous populations") that had to be studied to determine the most appropriate public health measures to control the spread of the virus once it was discovered to be the causative agent. It is like a wooden wheel, with its hub (those already infected – the prevalence rate) and the spokes that distribute the disease in a variety of ways within a circumscribed community.

That brings us face to face with the question about the incidence and prevalence of the disease as these factors have a significant role to play in the spread of the infection and the rapidity of its penetration into any society. This alerted the researchers to the fact that HIV infection is mostly a sexually transmitted disease and if you put together a society where the prevalence rate is high and there is widespread sexual promiscuity, then you find that the incidence rate rapidly escalates and you have a major epidemic on your hands. If you then consider another variable, notably the ease of travel between different societies (along the axle linking one wheel to another wheel or community) and maintain a promiscuous lifestyle between the mixing populations, then a pandemic is inevitable.

The epidemiologists will have a field day of interesting data to analyse with their smart computers but the politicians will have a monstrous nightmare.

Now turn your attention to the different populations of patients found to contract the disease. Take those who get the disease from contaminated blood transfusions or blood products. How did we deal with the problem? We developed a test to detect the virus in donated blood and in potential blood donors. The homosexual community was advised not to become blood donors. But you were left with a residue of HIV positive people who had been innocently infected by being given infected blood.

What has happened to this residual population? How many are now dead? How many people did they infect through sexual intercourse? How many sexual partners have been followed? What do we know about them?

As you move from one population of HIV positive persons to another population, you will find that there is a complex of factors or variables that contribute to the spread of AIDS in any particular society and the relative importance of such factors will determine the strategy best suited for that population. The population of intravenous drug users requires us to modify the drug taking behaviour of these people and this is further complicated by the intrusion of Hepatitis C into the equation of policy formation.

But across all populations, one factor is always profoundly important and that is sexual behaviour. This is why the African question is so profoundly disturbing.

Shelton with the help of others working in Africa, advanced the concept of 10 myths and one truth:

Ten myths and one truth about generalised HIV epidemic (James D. Shelton)

Despite substantial progress against AIDS worldwide, we are still losing ground. The number of new infections continues to dwarf the numbers who start anti-retroviral therapy in developing countries. Most infections occur in widespread or generalised epidemics in heterosexuals in just a few countries in southern and eastern Africa. Although HIV incidence has fallen in Uganda, Kenya, and Zimbabwe, the generalised epidemic rages on. Something is not working. Ten misconceptions impede prevention.

1. **HIV spreads like wildfire**: Typically it does not. HIV is very infectious in the first weeks when virus levels are high, but not in the subsequent many-year quiescent phase. Only about 8 per cent of people whose primary heterosexual partners have the virus become infected each year. Thus Kenya has more couples in which only one person is infected than couples in which both are (figure). This low

infectiousness in heterosexual relationships partly explains why HIV has spared most of the world's populations. However, the exceptional generalised epidemics in Africa seem largely driven by concurrent partnerships, in which some people have more than one regular partner. This pattern allows rapid dissemination when a new infection is introduced and probably involves more frequent risky sex than in sporadic or exclusive relationships.

2. **Sex work is the problem**: Formal sex work is uncommon in these generalised epidemics. In Lesotho, fewer than 2 per cent of men reported paying for sex in the previous year, although 29 per cent reported multiple partners. Nuanced economic support is an important enabler of regular concurrent partnerships and transactional sex, but the targeting of sex work in prevention campaigns has limited usefulness.

3. **Men are the problem**: The behaviour of men, including cross-generational and coercive sex, contributes substantially to the establishment of generalised epidemics. But a heterosexual epidemic requires some women to have multiple partners. The importance of women in generalised epidemics is evidenced by the high proportion (sometimes the majority) of discordant couples in which the woman, not the man, is HIV positive.

4. **Adolescents are the problem**: Generalised epidemics span all reproductive ages. Although adolescent women are affected through sex with older men, HIV incidence increases in women in their 20s and later in life. Men are infected at even older ages. Thus interventions in young

people, including abstinence, although important, have limited usefulness.

5. **Poverty and discrimination are the problem**: These factors can surely engender risky sex. But HIV is paradoxically more common in wealthier people than in poorer people, perhaps because wealth and mobility support concurrent sexual partnerships. Moreover, HIV has declined without major improvements in poverty and discrimination, notably in Zimbabwe (notwithstanding substantial economic and social distress).

6. **Condom use, especially by sex workers, is crucial** to the containment of concentrated epidemics, and condoms help to protect some individuals. But condoms alone have limited impact in generalised epidemics. Many people dislike using them (especially in regular relationships), protection is imperfect, use is often irregular, and condoms seem to foster disinhibition, in which people engage in risky sex either with condoms or with the intention of using condoms.

7. **HIV testing is the answer**: That learning one's HIV status (hopefully with counselling) should lead to behavioural change and reduced risk seems intuitive. However, real-world evidence of such change is discouraging, especially for the large majority who test negative. Moreover any changes must be sustained for years. And very newly infected people, who are highly infectious, do not yet test HIV positive.

8. **Treatment is the answer**: Theoretically, treatment and

counselling might aid prevention by lowering viral levels (and infectiousness) in those treated, reducing denial about HIV, and promoting behavioural change. However, no clear effect has emerged. Indeed these salutary effects might be outweighed by negative effects, such as resumption of sexual activity once those on anti-retroviral feel well, and disinhibition when people realise that HIV might no longer be a death sentence.

9. **New technology is the answer**: Many resources are devoted to vaccines, microbicides, and prophylactic anti-retroviral. Unfortunately any success appears to be far off. Moreover, such innovations might be mainly targeted only at very high-risk populations, rely on behavioural compliance, and engender disinhibition. Similarly, treatment of sexually transmitted infections to prevent HIV has been disappointing. Even male circumcision, an already available, unmistakably effective, and compelling priority will take years to have additional substantial effect.

10. **Sexual behaviour will not change**: Actually, facing the prospect of deadly illness, many people will change. Homosexual men in the USA radically changed behaviour in the 1980s. And the reductions in HIV incidence in Kenya and eastern Zimbabwe were accompanied by large drops in multiple partners, probably largely as a spontaneous reaction to fear.

Truthfully, our priority must be on the key driver of generalised epidemics – concurrent partnerships. Although many people sense that multiple partners are risky, they do not realise the particular risk of concurrent partnerships. Indeed, technical appreciation of their role is recent.[6] But partner limitation has also been neglected because of the culture wars between advocates of condoms and advocates of abstinence, because it smacks of moralising, because mass behavioural change is alien to most medical professionals, and because of the competing priorities of HIV programmes.

Fortunately we can enhance partner-limitation behaviour, akin to the behaviour change that many people have adopted spontaneously. State-of-the-art behaviour-change techniques, including explicit messages, that are sensitive to local cultures, can raise perception of personalised risk. Even modest reductions in concurrent partnerships could substantially dampen the epidemic dynamic. Other prevention approaches also have merit, but they can be much more effective in conjunction with partner-limitation.

Now, more than 20 years into HIV prevention, we have to get it right.

I thank Daniel Halperin and Willard Cates for helpful ideas on this Comment. My views here are not necessarily those of USAID. I declare that I have no conflict of interest. (J. Shelton).

A commentary (JNS)

Out of all this, in the fields of science and medical ethics, we come back to the questions of condoms, needle exchange programmes, professional duties and intellectual honesty. There is no need to discuss theology or dogmatic religious beliefs and in fact Benedict did not do so. He seems to have been well briefed by workers in the African field.

He alluded to scientific evidence from the grass roots of the AIDS epidemic in Africa; he was concerned about the debasement of human sexuality and the status of women in many African societies. He was concerned about the concept of the common good and the value systems of many Western societies. He was concerned about poverty and the slow development of educational standards in third world countries. He was outspoken about the manner in which the first world channeled its money into so-called programmes of aid for underdeveloped regions of the world.

What he did not mention was the scandalous behaviour of the media and of those with vested interests in the field of medical science. Nor did he comment about the manner in which public debate is conducted and about the censorship that is perpetrated to stifle the presentation of opinions not held by the "academic elite".

The capture by the secular forces of radical feminism, the radical environmentalists and the homosexual lobby, not to mention the strident atheists, of key posts in the media, the universities, the colleges, and in major political parties, has resulted in a confusion of values across several generations. This was always designed to shape public opinion, in a largely uncritical world of adolescence released from inhibitions and imbued with a false sense of freedom and tolerance. The older generations are gradually losing their religious beliefs as these have been eliminated from formal education or perverted by New Age hermeneutics mixed in the cauldron of sexual permissiveness, drug taking and heavy alcohol consumption.

Epilogue (JNS): 7 April 2013

It is worth mentioning that Edward Green has occupied several important international posts as he examined the AIDS epidemic in sub-Saharan Africa. In 2003, he published a book called *Rethinking AIDS Prevention* in which he set out trenchant commentaries on the misguided premises of the AIDS authorities running the programmes in Africa. An even more devastating critique is his later book, released in 2011 – *Broken Promises: How the AIDS Establishment has Betrayed the Developing World*. A review of that book can be found on the website of *Mercator Net*, written by a journalist Dale O'Leary (22 July 2011). It is a very powerful indictment of the structures of the "entrenched AIDS establishment" and I am surprised that nobody has ever suggested that it should be closely scrutinised by an independent Royal Commission or its equivalent international organisation.

O'Leary's review should be closely studied as an introduction to so-called *"evidence-based medicine."*

As one widens the scope of thinking about the ultimate truth of our universe, one needs to turn one's attention to the subject of what we mean by "evidence". In another context, I came across an essay which I wrote after reading an article by Andrew Bolt. The essay is reproduced in its entirety in the next chapter. As the language is at times technical, it is preceded by a glossary of terms and an introductory preamble.

2

Drug abuse and evidence based medicine

Glossary of terms

Epidemiology:

From Basic Epidemiology by the World Health Organization.

Epidemiology has been defined as "the study of the distribution and (the) determinants of health related states or events in specified populations, and the application of this study to control of 'health problems'".

The target of such a study is a human population.

A population:

A population means a group of people who are pooled together because they share a common factor at the commencement of the study. It may be because they share a common geographical area such as the city of Melbourne or the suburb of Frankston, or they have a particular disease, such as hypertension or AIDS, or are being treated with a drug for a particular disease. The whole population may be studied or a representative sample of suitable size.

An epidemiological study:

There are two main types of epidemiological studies.

1. An experimental study. This approach is easier in animals than in humans as it requires strict ethical considerations especially informed consent. In this type of study the investigator has control of some factor which can be followed in a predetermined way in two matched populations. In the disease of AIDS, the factor being tested could be the use of condoms as opposed to their non-use. It presupposes that the two populations are homogeneous. It leads in the direction of randomised controlled trials.

2. An observational study is one where the investigator does not have adequate control over the factor or the population, to the extent that a cause and effect relationship cannot be safely assumed. This raises the question of homogeneous and heterogeneous populations.

Homogeneous and heterogeneous opulations:

When comparing two populations of people and the introduction of a common factor (or variable), one must be conscious of other factors that may contribute to a particular outcome, such as the disease AIDS. For example, if one population has a very promiscuous sexual lifestyle and the other does not, the use rate of condoms may be the same but the outcome of an HIV infection can vary significantly. The investigator must have adequate control of the use rate of condoms and be sure that the sexual behaviour of the two populations is the same.

In recent times, observational studies have dominated the

field of epidemiological research. The main essay discusses these problems.

Robust and soft data:

When trying to analyse any relationship between a variable (like condom use) and an outcome like the disease of AIDS, the investigator must be sure that the data that he collects is accurate. If you rely on self-reporting, the data is "soft" since one cannot be sure that it has been truthfully imparted or accurately recalled. It is subject to a variety of biased information. It is known as "soft data." On the other hand, when the data can be objectively verified and any bias eliminated, the data base is recognised as "robust".

Advocacy research:

This is a new term introduced to categorise research designed to serve an ideological or political cause.

Preamble

In the debate about public policy to combat the AIDS epidemic, one is left with the enigma of "evidence-based medicine". The controversial feature writer in the *Herald Sun*, Andrew Bolt, wrote an interesting article which appeared on 17 April 2009.

What Bolt showed was that journalists, using identical comments made by two political opponents (Bush and Obama), can opine in opposite directions depending on their own political preferences: "So what do we conclude from all this? That all humans tend to see only what reinforces their prejudices. That even newspaper editors are no better. That given this, debate is essential if we are to learn all sides of any argument."

This is a phenomenon that has also been observed in the scientific literature as is outlined in this essay on evidence-based medicine.

Shared needles

In the *Sunday Herald Sun* (6 May 2007), an article was highlighted as DIAL-a-NEEDLE. This was followed by an editorial commenting as follows: "Yes there are good reasons to provide a needle service. The sharing of needles is a health hazard. It promotes the spread of AIDS. Protecting drug addicts from themselves is a noble goal and we are all for it."

A week before that editorial appeared, at an international drug conference, I drew attention to problems associated with modern day scientific research. It is apparent from the editorial in the *Sunday Herald Sun* that many government instrumentalities in the field of drug abuse continue to act on policies that are based on very suspect premises and poor methodologies. This is particularly true on the policies of needle exchange programmes and medically supervised injecting rooms.

But it is not peculiar to drug abuse for it is manifest in many disciplines of scientific endeavour. Much of the debate about climate change is a debate about methodology, confounding variables, computer modelling, statistical formulae and even basic premises. The problem impinges on the questions of ethical behaviour, the moulding of public opinion and the concept of the common good as opposed to the vested interests of the scientific community or a political lobby.

Historical introduction

It was in the early 1980s that I began to take a critical interest in medical research. It was a time when reproductive technology burst on the scene and captured the public imagination. Louise Brown was born in July 1978, although the technology had its early development in the veterinary sciences. This scientific achievement resulted in the formation in Australia of the Monash Bioethics Centre which was initially funded by the National Health and Medical Research Council. This centre, directed by Professor Peter Singer, prompted the formation of other bioethics centres, both in Australia and abroad as the community began to struggle over the question of ethical principles that should govern scientific research. Of course, the issue had earlier been addressed in the Nuremberg Code of 1949 and the Declaration of Helsinki in 1964. There are several documents of the United Nations that appeared in the middle of the 20th century that laid down fundamental bioethical principles. Research institutes were advised to establish Institutional Ethics Committees but little appeared that could be applied to the field of drug abuse.

However, drug abuse, especially in the Western world emerged as a major public health issue in the 1960s and with it there appeared many research papers and commentaries that revealed the impact of ideological overtones and a struggle to find a formula to determine national drug policy. In several countries of the Western world, books and articles were written by political activists, both on the right and the left of politics, that sought to influence not only national policy but international agreements. Many organisations were launched, often heavily backed by large sums of money, with opposing philosophies, and both sides claimed that justice should prevail, based on sound scientific evidence.

Various professional disciplines became involved – public health officers, physicians, nurses, social workers and sociologists, psychologists, criminologists, the legal profession, law enforcement officers, government advisory bodies, and religious organisations. All marshalled evidence-based on their particular area of expertise. Their advocacy of a platform of measures to deal with the use of so-called illegal drugs was often heralded as evidence-based and so arose my interest in the quality of that evidence.

Most of the evidence is found in scientific journals, proceedings of conferences, official reports of government bodies and non-government organisations (NGOs), annual reports and review articles in lay and scientific journals and newspapers. Often the "evidence" becomes incorporated into textbooks and printed materials used for public education and policy decisions.

A great deal of this material can be accessed on the internet or online services of various institutions. *Medline* is a well-known service of such a nature.

But how reliable are all these sources?

In papers published in scientific journals, the authors and editors follow a certain format, popularly known as IMRaD – Introduction, Methods, Research and Discussion. When the paper is submitted, the editor will send the article for peer review and the paper is returned to the editor with the reviewer's comments. The final decision rests with the editor. This process of research and the communication of its findings has been the accepted norm for a long period of time and millions of papers using this format have been published in an expanding field of journal development. At first sight, this appears to be an excellent way of presenting a scientific paper but in the last 25 years, there has developed significant scepticism about what actually happens in practice.

Peer review and editorial decisions

In a recent issue of the *Journal of the Royal Society of Medicine* (December 2006), there appeared an article entitled "Scientific Journals are 'faith based': is there science behind peer review?" The article commented: "Jefferson recently presented an outstanding review of peer review and could find only 19 studies on peer review that were scientifically sound. We could find only 14 articles examining the editorial board/editorial decision making. Thus, with over 50 million articles and 300 years of traditional journal approaches, there has been only a handful of studies questioning or testing the journal process itself." The article further commented that "[r]ecent studies reveal that peer review often misses major methodological problems in articles."

It is a well-known fact that editors of scientific journals reveal a bias (publication bias) towards the publication of results that show a "statistical significance". Those articles are more likely to appear in the scientific journals than articles that reveal no "positive outcome". This becomes most important when researchers conduct a literature review as they will fail to detect papers that have been rejected for publication. This also applies in the reverse direction when studies that reveal a significant outcome are not published when the finding is inconvenient for the "politically correct".

The questions of peer review and editorial selection are well recognised and international conferences are now held on these very subjects. One of the major contributors to such conferences is Douglas G. Altman, an internationally acclaimed biostatistician and epidemiologist who wrote as follows in the *Journal of the American Medical Association* (2002; 287: 2765-2767): "A study should not mislead; otherwise it could adversely affect clinical practice and future research." In 1994 I observed that research papers commonly contain methodological errors, report selectively, and draw unjustified conclusions.

Methodology covers such items as study design, selecting, collecting and recording data, analysis of the data and the choice of a statistical package.

Meta-analysis

For a variety of reasons, Altman's admonition can escape the scrutiny of peer review and this is well described in the scientific literature. Of particular interest are the questions of methodology, especially the use of meta-analysis and ecological studies, together with the complex statistical formulae that are used to deal with confounding variables. Confounding variables are factors that can affect the outcome of a study but are either not included or considered in the study design or information about them is not available in the data used for the study. For example, if we study the relationship between the use of needle exchange programmes and the incidence of HIV but do not know the sexual behaviour of the populations being compared, there is a significant variable that is being overlooked and which will "confound" any apparent association between needle programmes and the incidence of

HIV. Such difficulties are well demonstrated in articles and reports that claim to evaluate needle exchange programmes, medically supervised injecting rooms, maintenance programmes and use tolerance of drug use.

Another issue is the question of the distinction between incidence and prevalence. If population (X) has a high prevalence rate of HIV at a time when it starts a new policy that does not include (needle exchange programmes (NEPs) (say 20 per cent) and after five years its prevalence rate of HIV falls to 16 per cent, it has a falling incidence rate over that period. On the other hand, if another population (Y) has a low prevalence rate (say 5 per cent) at the beginning of a programme using NEPs and at the end of five years its prevalence rate is 8 per cent, all other factors being equal, its incidence rate will have risen but its prevalence rate at the time of comparison will be much lower than in population (X). At the point of comparison, if you do not know the respective incidence rates, you will draw a wrong conclusion about the effectiveness of the programmes in controlling HIV infections. This constitutes a confounding variable.

The majority of scientists and readers of scientific journals are not proficient in their knowledge about biostatistics, epidemiological principles, appropriate biostatistical applications and what constitutes hard or soft evidence.

This applies also to the discernment of confounding variables that may affect the data when meta-analysis is done. In an article in the *British Medical Journal* in 1994, D.G. Altman, wrote as follows: "What should we think about researchers who use the wrong techniques (either wilfully or in ignorance) use the right techniques wrongly, misinterpret their results, report their results selectively, cite the literature selectively, and draw unjustified conclusions? We should be appalled. Yet numerous studies of the medical literature, in both general and specialist journals have shown that the above phenomena are common."

The picture is further complicated when premises, based on the analysis, are adopted for the evaluation of costs, benefits and outcomes. Virtually all these studies are based on the epidemiological device of meta-analysis, a statistical tool that has become very popular in the drug field. Theoretically, meta-analysis sounds a very reasonable methodology, especially when it is very difficult and very costly to conduct randomised controlled trials with sufficient numbers of patients or clients. So we need to understand the method and the present controversy over its use and application.

Meta-analysis is a statistical technique for combining the data and findings of independent studies that seem to deal with a common hypothesis or research question. An outstanding example in the field of Drug Abuse is the *Evaluation of NEPs*. There are numerous studies published in the journals, across a broad range of disciplines. They usually deal with small numbers of clients and try to study a relatively simple question, which can be affected by many variables, some of which are confounding variables. The classical example is the *Effect of NEPS on the Incidence of HIV Infection in Injecting Drug Users* (IDUs). A very legitimate question. Here are three commentaries.

1. After reviewing all of the research to date, the senior scientists of the Department and I have unanimously

agreed that there is conclusive scientific evidence that syringe exchange programmes, as part of a comprehensive HIV prevention strategy, are an effective public health intervention that reduces the transmission of HIV and does not encourage the use of illegal drugs (U.S. Surgeon-General Dr. David Satcher, Department of Health and Human Services, 2000).

2. Early in the course of this pandemic, it seemed that needle/ syringe exchange programmes might provide an effective intervention in the growing epidemic of HIV disease among drug injectors but hard evidence to show this is lacking. Without credible evidence of efficacy, the provision of clean needles and syringes appears primarily to support the individual's addiction and alongside with it, drug related high-risk sexual behaviour. (An Evidence-based Review of Needle Exchange Programmes by Dr. F.J. Payne, formerly a medical epidemiologist with the Centers for Disease Control and former Senior Research Epidemiologist with the National Institute of Health and now Medical Advisor to the Children's AIDS Fund.

3. Many drug prevention experts have long feared that the proliferation of NEPs, now numbering over a 100 in the U.S. would result in a rise in heroin use, and indeed this has come to pass. This rise in drug use was ignored by all the federally funded studies which recommended federally funding NEPs. The National Center on Addiction and Substance Abuse at Columbia University reported on 14 August 1997 that heroin use by American teens doubled

from 1991 to 1996. In the past decade, experts estimate that the number of U.S. heroin addicts has risen from 550,000 to 700,000. (Janet Lapley MD, "Commentary on 1998 Report on Needle Exchange Programmes in the U.S.A.", Reproduced in *Drugs Dilemma*, 2000).

Problems with meta-analysis

These three scientists reviewed the studies using meta-analysis of data in the course of doing literature searches. The conflict of opinions is the outcome of the selection process of the relevant data and the heterogeneity of the populations being studied. By heterogeneity is meant that there are significant differences in the populations under study (including the methodology) which need to be known and taken into account when analysing the findings. An important principle of good meta-analysis is the complete coverage of all relevant studies (both published in peer reviewed journals or elsewhere) and an assessment of the robustness of each study in supporting the conclusions of the author(s).

Another important principle is the quality of the data. Payne makes the point that much of the data collected in the NEP studies is based on the self-reporting of the intravenous drug users. He observes: "The reliability of self-reported behaviour by addicts is always open to question under the best of circumstances."

A final point about meta-analysis is the question of the statistical packages that are used to arrive at a sound interpretation of the data when confounding variables must be accommodated. At this point, most readers of these articles are at the mercy of the statisticians who alone have the necessary expertise to determine the best formula. Moreover it is not simply a question of excluding the possibility of chance but also of establishing the credibility and integrity of the conclusions.

Ecological studies

Ecological studies are about populations of peoples and such studies have an inbuilt fallacy. The Report, *Return on Investment and Syringe Programs in Australia* (2002), under the aegis of the Department of Health and Ageing, is an ecological study. Very few people, including members of the medical profession, know anything about such studies.

The study entailed a comparison of data in Australia with data from 41-67 cities in Asia, Europe, North America, South America, the United Kingdom, and New Zealand. This was a formidable task. In the Executive Summary, it stated: "The analysis found that cities that introduced NEPs had a mean annual 16.6 per cent decrease in HIV seroprevalence, compared with a mean annual 8.1 per cent increase in HIV seroprevalence in cities that had never introduced NSPs."

Then followed a very complex description of the statistical methodology which in itself requires comment by an independent biostatistician. Having reached its conclusions, premises were then established to determine a significant cost-benefit equation in favour of the Australian programme on NEPs.

My reaction at the time was that it did not make sense, that the populations were heterogeneous on several scores. I needed help from other sources. None of my medical colleagues knew about ecological studies, much less anything about the methodology.

Those in the field of epidemiology commented that there were problems with ecological analyses, especially when used in comparing data from many countries.

WHO, in its publication *Basic Epidemiology* (1994), stated: "Although easy to conduct and thus attractive, ecological studies are often difficult to interpret since it is seldom possible to examine directly the various potential explanations for findings."

For a long time, only after I read through many studies using meta-analysis and several cohort studies did it dawn on me that the populations could easily have been heterogeneous. In those cities in which needle exchange programmes had been introduced, there had probably occurred sizeable influxes of young IDUs, with low prevalence rates for HIV and Hepatitis C Virus (HCV) which diluted the overall prevalence rates for those diseases in the total population of IDUs.

Instead of NEPs affecting the incidence rate for HIV and HCV, the NEPs merely expanded the population of IDUs, attracting younger users and more females. All the cohort studies in the NEPs centres revealed this phenomenon and over time these new users became HCV positive. HIV prevalence also rose but mainly due to promiscuous sexual behaviour. The cohort study in Baltimore, conducted by the National Institute for Drug Abuse revealed that sexual behaviour was the main determinant of HIV infection and the continued high rate of needle/syringe sharing was mainly responsible for HCV transmission.

The other problem that emerged was the continued sharing of needles and syringes. Moreover in the cohort studies it was apparent that differences also existed in the ancillary services offered by the needle exchange centres. In the seminal paper by Hurley et al, the interpretation reads as follows: "Despite the possibility of confounding, our results, together with the clear theoretical mechanisms by which NEPs could reduce HIV incidence, strongly support the view that NEPs are effective." In fact the methodology is highly complex and the interpretation is not congruent with some of the cohort studies reviewed by F.J. Payne.

The article by Hurley et al was peer reviewed but in retrospect it should be reappraised by experienced biostatisticians not linked to the international harm reduction movement.

As ecological studies are population studies, such variables as cultural differences, socio-economic factors, sexual behaviours, ages and sexes, the basic prevalence rates at the time of entry, the expansion of the numbers of IDUs, the rate of needle sharing, the incidence rate and other variables are either unknown or not analysable. What follows therefore are inferences of causality derived from aggregated data, but not proof of causality. If then you assume that the NEPs are the true cause of the differences in the spread of HIV in the two general populations, you have used an unproven premise to construct a cost-benefit estimate.

The ecological fallacy

The ecological fallacy consists of inferring that there is a causal relationship between the provision of NEPs and a lowering of HIV and HCV infections in IDUs. As D.A. Freedman states: "It is all too easy to draw incorrect conclusions from aggregate data" (*Technical Report*, No 549, October 1999).

The inference drawn in the above document may be true but

it is not proven by the methodology of ecological studies. The observations of A.J. Payne, as reported above, suggest that the inference is not true. The real gold standard suggesting causality is a randomised controlled trial, a very difficult trial to mount, given the nature of the population to be studied.

As reported in the *New England Journal of Medicine* (1997; 337: 536-542) by Lelorier et al, when controlled trials were done, 35 per cent of the matched meta-analyses were wrong in their predictions.

Piers Ackerman, writing in the *Sydney Daily Telegraph* (2 May 2007), commented on the *Evaluation of the Sydney Medically Supervised Injecting Room*. Contrary to the Report published by the evaluators, an independent study of the data used in the evaluation revealed that the centre had proved to be an abject failure and should have been closed at the end of the trial period.

There are many lessons to be learned from these experiences and most of them have been spelt out in the scientific literature. In recent years, considerable scepticism has been expressed about the present state of peer reviewed journals, mainly due to the emergence of ideological factors and vested interests of researchers and sponsors. The development of modern day computers has transformed the field of research, with their enormous power to crunch numbers, with their packages of statistical analyses and their power to do literature searches. In many fields, computer modelling has become awe-inspiring and at the same time highly suspect.

The situation has now developed where readers of these communications must exercise great caution and critical judgment when reading any paper or document or newspaper article, no matter where it is published. It is wise to have available as a consultant, an independent biostatistician, with no vested interest, both to give an opinion on any paper or document or to assist in the design of any study in the field of research. One must know the vested interests of authors and sponsors and often one needs to know the identities of those who do peer reviews.

One needs to scrutinise the references and sources of information and there will be times when one needs to have access to the raw data of the research that has been done.

Evidence-based Medicine

As the doyen of the concept of *evidence-based medicine*, David Sacket has said, "The honorary degree of *Sackettisation* is defined as 'the artificial linkage of a publication to the evidence-based medicine movement in order to improve sales'." (*BMJ*, 2000;320:1283)

The editorial comment on NEPs in the *Sunday Herald Sun* was not based on evidential proof.

3

The effectiveness of condoms in the AIDS epidemic

Part One: Scientific Aspects

There are several web sites on the internet that are valuable sources of information. One such site is the WHO Reproductive Health Library (RHL). Below is an excerpt that is most helpful in understanding the problems that are intrinsic to the studies about condom use in the prevention of HIV transmission.

As one pursues the references associated with this site, one begins to suspect that *The Lancet* editorial advocating the redemption of the Pope has been turned on its head. Is there any redemption possible for UNAIDS?

The article below is an excerpt from the RHL.

Condom effectiveness in reducing heterosexual HIV transmission

RHL Commentary is by David Wilkinson whose comments are directed to a *Cochrane Review* conducted by Weller et al.

The Cochrane review to which Wilkinson refers is also published by WHO and appears on its website. Cochrane reviews trace the research studies that have been published in a wide-ranging literature search and then analyses them to assess the soundness of their methodology and of the inferences drawn by their authors.

A review seeks out the sound evidence that will assist in healthcare policy formation. The source of this review is Weller, S.C. and Davis-Beaty, K., "Condom effectiveness in reducing heterosexual HIV transmission". Cochrane Database of Systematic Reviews, 2002, Issue 1, Art, No. CD003255. DOI: 1002/14651858. CD 003255. (JNS).

Evidence summary (David Wilkinson)

This Cochrane review (Weller et al) is an excellent attempt to estimate the effectiveness of condom use in reducing heterosexual transmission of HIV. While several studies have looked at this issue, many of these have been small, and the reviews done to date have had a number of methodological problems associated with them.

The authors of the Cochrane review identified and selected 14 studies involving discordant couples (i.e., couples in which one of the partners is HIV positive and the other free from HIV). A total of 587 people who reported "always" using condoms during sexual intercourse, and 276 people who reported "never" using condoms were included in these studies.

The incidence of HIV infection among those who reported always using condoms was 1.14 per 100 person-years (95 per cent confidence interval 0.56-2.04), while it was 5.75 per 100 person-years (95 per cent CI 3.16-9.66) among those who never used them. This gave an 80 per cent reduction in the incidence of infection with condom use.

It is important to note, however, two important limitations: (a) the meta-analysis was done using data from observational studies;

and (b) the authors did not provide confidence intervals for their estimated effect of 80 per cent.

This is a well done review. As the authors correctly point out, it is logistically and ethically impossible to do randomised controlled trials to find out whether condom use reduces the risk of HIV transmission. As such, we have to rely on observational studies. The studies used in this review typically compare rates of HIV infection in groups of people who report always or never using condoms. Observational studies inherently carry a risk of bias as people make choices for reasons, and if the choice about using condoms or not is related to other risk factors for HIV, then the estimate of effect that we get will be inaccurate.

So, in this study, in spite of the best efforts of the authors, we can't be sure that condoms really reduce HIV incidence by 80 per cent. It may be, for example, that people who use condoms always also practice safe sex and have fewer partners, thereby reducing their HIV risk irrespective of condom use. It might also be that some people who report always using condoms do not actually do so but tell the researchers that they do in order to "look good". Similar points could be made about people reporting not using condoms. Self-reported data always have the risk of being unreliable; and in this case there is no other means of confirming the findings.

If we take the extreme values from the 95 per cent confidence intervals of the HIV incidence rates reported in the two cohorts, we find that condom use may be associated with reduced HIV incidence of between 94 per cent and 35 per cent. The wide range of values is explained by the small numbers of people

(863) and HIV infections (51) in the studies. Concurrent use of other measures could also contribute to this variation. As a result, the estimate of the incidence of HIV in the two groups is fairly imprecise (between 0.56 and 2.04 per 100 person-years for users, and between 3.16 and 9.66 per 100 person-years for non-users).

This lack of precision is not the fault of the authors and their review. It is an inherent feature of the available studies. As such, it is not really appropriate to estimate condom effectiveness at 80 per cent. While 80 per cent is the best single estimate of effectiveness, it is also fair to say that the true measure of the effect could be as low as 35 per cent or as high as 94 per cent, as the authors state in the review.

This document should be cited as: David Wilkinson, "Condom effectiveness in reducing heterosexual HIV transmission: RHL commentary" (last revised: 11 November 2002. The WHO Reproductive Health Library, No. 9, Update Software Ltd, Oxford, 2006.

Commentary (JNS)

It should be noted that the research on the control of the spread of AIDS has inherent problems that makes it virtually impossible to express with dogmatic certainty what is the role of the use of condoms in preventing the transmission of HIV infection.

Wilkinson starts by saying that it is logistically and ethically impossible to conduct randomised controlled trials to determine the effectiveness of condoms. It is one thing to postulate that condoms are very effective in the prevention of AIDS (the hypothesis) but it is ethically improper to try and do it by the gold standard of epidemiological research and to expose subjects to the possibility of contracting a fatal disease. There are many facets to the ethics of scientific research and there is the added problem of informed consent.

Logistically there are so many variables to be considered and the populations of people at risk are so diverse (heterogeneous) that it is very difficult to generalise across all populations. To say categorically that "the East-West Centre in Hawaii has estimated that if condom use had not been widely promoted and adopted, today eight million Thais would be infected rather than the 550,000 now living with the virus," is, to say the least, very misleading (M. Toole and R. Moodie). "Five years into the (Thai) campaign only 12 per cent of the Thai military conscripts reported visiting a sex worker, down from 60 per cent five years earlier" (Toole & Moodie again). Was this an effect of condom use or was it an effect of education and changed sexual behaviour? How was the cost-benefit analysis done? (see Mike Toole & Rob Moodie: "The Evidence on preventing AIDS is clear", 14 April 2009. Internet search).

This is where it becomes important for neutral reviewers to study the original papers or documents to determine the quality and robustness of the study or report, and to observe whether the inferences match the data or are compromised by the author(s)' prejudices. Has there been a selective choice of studies to match the prejudices of the authors? It is interesting to quote the extract below which has been reproduced from the exemplary Cochrane review commented upon by Wilkinson:

Because observational studies may be biased by an unequal

distribution of HIV risk factors across study categories, the following variables were recorded when available: direction of transmission (male-to-female or female-to male), date of study and subject enrollment, source of infection in the index case (IDU, blood product recipient , bisexual , heterosexual), level of infectivity in the index case, type of condom used (latex or other type), the presence or history of another STI in the partner, circumcision in male partners, subtype of HIV, estimates of frequency of sexual intercourse, length of sexual relationship, age, and country. (See data collection form in Appendix B). Quality of studies was estimated by the detail and specificity in available data.

The authors of the *Cochrane Review* (S. Weller & K. Davis-Beaty) cannot even be sure of the figure of 80 per cent effectiveness across all populations. Wilkinson points out that it could be as low as 35 per cent in some study groups.

There are two problems with the *Cochrane Review*, one of which is not due to the researchers. It is due to the fact that there seems to be no good longitudinal study of a cohort of the discordant spouses of those who contracted the disease from blood transfusions or blood products early in the study of HIV infections. How many of that original "cohort" of innocent victims of blood transmission are alive and how many of their monogamous spouses are still disease-free? Theoretically this cohort offers the best opportunity to gain an insight into the effectiveness of condom use if there is a good data base.

The second problem is on the margins of the epidemic. It is the question of the effectiveness of condom use as a contraceptive.

The fact is that a woman has fertile and infertile phases in her monthly periods and pregnancy only occurs when the timing of intercourse is within the fertile part of the cycle (see *The Billings Method* by Westmore and Billings). The use of condoms in the infertile time has no causal association.

This *Cochrane Review* is the single most important document to be found on a literature search of the effectiveness of condoms. And yet it is not mentioned by any of the scientists who have attacked the Pope for his comments about the epidemic in Africa. When one observes who these scientists are and what positions they hold in the field of the transmission of the AIDS virus, one is drawn to a recent editorial and accompanying article in the *Journal of the Royal Society of Medicine* (Vol. 102, No. 2, February 2009).

In the article "The Fallacy of Impartiality: competing interest bias in academic publications", the authors Richard Smith et al conclude as follows: "Our message is simple: we must recognise that we are all conflicted and declare accordingly. A view of the world that sees employees of private-for-profit companies as conflicted, and doctors, or employees of public and academic bodies, as not, is naïve, potentially deceptive and likely to distort reader response to new information."

One of the references to that article was another article published in the *British Medical Journal*: Montagu D., "Response to: The writing is on the wall for UNAIDS" (2008; 336: 1072-3). It is a review of UNAIDS by Roger England, Chairman, Health Systems Workshop, Grenada. The final paragraph is scathing:

Putting HIV in its place among other priorities will be resisted strongly. The global HIV industry is too big and

out of control. We have created a monster with too many
vested interests and reputations at stake, too many single
issue NGOs (in Mozambique, 100 NGOs are devoted
to HIV for every one concerned with maternal and child
health), too many relatively well paid HIV staff in affected
countries, and too many rock stars with AIDS support as
a fashion accessory. But until we do put HIV in its place,
countries will not get the delivery systems they need, and
switching $10 billion from HIV to support general health
budgets would make a big difference – roughly doubling
health workers' salaries in the whole of sub-Saharan Africa,
for example (or trebling them, if you don't include South
Africa).

Remember what the Pope said:

I would say that one cannot overcome this problem of
AIDS (in Africa) only with money – which is important,
but if there is no soul, no people who know how to use it,
(money) doesn't help.

One cannot overcome the problem with the distribution of
condoms. On the contrary, they increase the problem. The
solution can only be a double one: first, a humanisation of
sexuality, that is, a spiritual human renewal that brings with
it a new way of behaving with one another; second, a true
friendship even and especially with those who suffer, and a
willingness to make personal sacrifices and to be with the
suffering. And these are factors that help and that result in
real and visible progress.

Part Two: The role of the media and academia in the AIDS controversy

The agitated pronouncements of the media, the journalists, the editors, the news readers, the online commentators, the experts marshalled to provide the pontifical comments about evidence-based medicine, the unmitigated judgments about religious dogmatism, were a grim reminder about the unprofessional behaviour of much modern journalism.

After the African visit of Pope Benedict XVI, a gathering of African students took place in Rome on 29 March 2009 to greet the Pope. The head of the committee of African students in Rome, Pierre Baba Mansare, commented: "(T)he event was organised after seeing the coverage of the Pope's visit in the media. Of the Holy Father's whole pastoral message, the Western media only focused on the statement about condoms with the purpose of starting a polemic" (*Zenit News Service*).

The messages of the former Pope's tour seemed to have escaped the Western media, just as the messages of his Regensberg address in 2006 were ignored in the furor that focused on his opening remarks about religion and terrorism. (see James Schall, *The Regensberg Lecture*, The St. Augustine Press, 2007). It is not easy to enter the public square of debate and dialogue when the media fails to grasp the whole field of engagement and there are many hazards and traps along the way, especially when it traverses the terrain of religious beliefs and values.

A hostile journalist during an interview is focussed on winning a point about which he/she feels strongly and will tend to interrupt

your choice of words and the development of your argument.
They often use challenging headlines to distort your argument,
as appeared in *The Lancet* about redeeming the Pope. They can
readily misquote you or interpret your comments in a misleading
fashion. They can unexpectedly confront you with third parties
who profess to be experts and move the argument laterally. On
radio or television or as a moderator in a debate, they will often
have the last say. And they can confront you with a hostile audience
or abrasive manners of speech.

Many journalists do an excellent job at presenting a programme
and are well informed and courteous. There are others who wisely
do not write on a subject that they have not researched adequately.
On the occasion of the Pope commenting about the AIDS
epidemic in Africa, the response of the media in the Western press
was by and large unintelligent and hostile.

Susie O'Brien, a feature writer for the *Herald Sun*, attacked
Cardinal George Pell when he supported the Pope's comments (14
April 2009):

> AIDS in sub-Saharan Africa and 1.5 million Africans die
> from the condition every year. Children are being born
> with a deadly, preventable virus. Wives are being infected
> by husbands because they don't have the means to protect
> themselves.

> But Pell would rather put his religious beliefs ahead of
> the health of these people. I can't understand the Catholic
> Church's obsession with birth control. It's not like
> prophylactics were around in Jesus's time and he took a set
> against them. If a cleric spoke out against the evils of seat

belts, he would be rightly ridiculed. This is no different. Condoms work. They save lives. Pell should look at the science before shooting off at the mouth.

This is an example of a journalist, writing authoritatively and abusively on a subject about which she seems to have inadequate knowledge. But she is not peculiar just on this issue for she also has problems when she tries to write about religion. It is not the Catholic Church that has an obsession with birth control but rather our modern secular society that desires free sexual behaviour without the other natural component of the sex act – the procreation of children. There are several basic documents of the teachings of the Catholic Church on human sexuality and fertility awareness but you can safely bet that the attacking journalists have never studied them.

This sort of writing is becoming the norm in the ideological debates of our time and is often found at its worst on internet blog sites. The origin of these problems is the modern day version of the secular mind which cannot cope with an unchanging moral code of conduct, much less with the concept of an ultimate judgment by a supreme intelligence. There is a belief among the secularists that religion has no rational foundations and has no place in political debates nor in the stratosphere of academia. Such secularists have an iconoclastic bent of mind that descends at times into irrational intolerance.

An opinion however formed is often equated with conscience and human rights. This allows the journalist to be dogmatic and authoritative. Who can argue against freedom of conscience, an unqualified human right or unfair discrimination? But the debate is lopsided and irrational, based on sophistry and tactical measures to win community support or to lull the opposition into a state of indifference. And always the journalists have the advantage for their comments are freely expressed but their challengers are frequently screened out of publication.

The media commands the high ground of forming public opinion. With the development of information technology and the popularity of television with its numerous modes of presentation and selection of information, the news presenters have a format in which they are well experienced in controlling the flow of the discussion. Many in the community largely rely on these sources and do not perceive that a subtle process may be at work to shape their opinions. The churches, especially those of Christian orientation, must be careful in this regard when debating in the public square. Their spokespersons must be familiar with the basic evidence and should exhibit a calm and competent confidence in a dialectical situation that may be highly charged with personal innuendoes.

At the moment, Christianity and Catholicism in particular are subjected to the most hostile attacks, even in countries where Christianity was largely responsible for the formation of the political and judicial systems that fostered the growth of democratic principles and human rights. In these nations, especially on the European landscape, the growth of secular forces has seen a rejection of Christian values and institutions, resulting in the election of anti-Christian governments. There is frequently a paradoxical shift to liberalism in government while the general population has not fully shed its Christian culture in the hearts of its members.

Among the attacks on the three main monotheistic religions of modern times are many vitriolic expressions of pure hatred and sheer intolerance of their existence. The concept of engaging in a rational dialogue between these countervailing philosophies has deteriorated to a point of imposing political solutions by winning electoral majorities or by controlling the judicial system.

Academia is an even more complex situation. The universities are mostly secular institutions, often with attached religious colleges. In the Western world, there are universities that are religious in orientation, some with pontifical recognition. In some countries, such as the U.S., there are tertiary colleges that provide courses in the fine arts, preparatory to graduating to universities that offer scientific faculties such as dentistry and medicine and veterinary science.

There are the teachers, the students and the institutions. The teachers are set in an hierarchical structure, with those in higher orders holding tenured positions in the various faculties of learning. The longer tenures are bequeathed to those who have been through a short period of trial or who have moved across from other institutions where they acquired expertise and an impressive curriculum vitae (CV) of achievements and published work. These tenured positions are much sought after as they carry status as learned professors and associates; they attract a substantial salary and preferment in funding from governments and research institutes and an opportunity to lecture worldwide. This adds to status and to one's CV. It also allows for consultations with one's peers and often for paid consultancies with government and public institutions.

Theoretically this is not a bad system and mostly it works quite well. It tends to come apart when the aura of the individual and the institutional faculty is stamped on other matters for which the individual has no special expertise, such as a scientist when he ventures into religious beliefs or the morality of scientific research. It is compounded when he distorts the evidence by selective use of published work or where he advises rejection of material which challenges his own interpretations of a contentious issue.

In the academic institutions and between institutions and at scientific conferences, discussion is often elitist and the language used is for professionals so that the community at large is mystified. This in-house conversation is not appropriate when it may determine political decisions or judicial outcomes, often involving large sums of public money as happened with the funding of embryonic stem cell research.

The effect on students is potentially transforming if ideological positions are promoted on matters that are in dispute. This happens with some aspects of political and social philosophy when presented without a comparable presentation of opposing philosophical viewpoints. The status of the lecturer vis-à-vis the student body may have a significant impact on opinion formation. Moreover there have been occasions when applicants for an academic post are rejected because their philosophical beliefs do not match those of the "establishment".

In academia, religion is viewed as incompatible with the scientific method and the evidence of empirical observations. Therefore the academics maintain that within the academy, religion should not be taught as a factor for consideration in any analysis of scientific propositions. I find this anomalous when one considers the approach adopted by Aristotle and the manner in which he applied his mind to seek the underlying reality of things as he observed the surrounding world in which he lived.

In academic institutions run by religious organisations such as the pontifical universities, the religious beliefs of the sponsoring body are open to study, not only as a faculty of the university but also as sources of learning that can be applied in any other faculty. In addition, such institutions provide religious services appropriate to the daily lives of those students who share the religious beliefs of the sponsoring organisation. In the Catholic Church, this means the availability of a pervading Catholic culture, with the sacrifice of the Mass, other liturgical practices and the administration of the sacraments.

Over the last three to four decades however, much controversy has taken place over the quality of religious teaching in Catholic universities and colleges as academic staff have adopted theological positions that are described as deviant or dissident.

This raises two questions for such Catholic institutions. In the first place is the question of funding by the secular government or non-government agencies, such as research institutes. It also raises the question of fundraising from non-government sources, such as philanthropic trusts and by personal bequests. The second is the external supervision of the theological and related faculties by delegated authorities when scholars venture into their interpretations of the teachings of the Catholic Church. There often arises a tension between the concept of "academic freedom" and the Church authorities responsible for protecting the Deposit of Faith. The mix of the secular sciences and the faculties of philosophy, bioethics and theology generate administrative issues in tertiary institutions that operate under the auspices of the Catholic Church.

These are questions that go beyond my archival musings and move us on to forward planning. In an age when technology has exploded beyond the old world of science fiction, we will have to review what it means to be truly human.

SECTION TWO

Politics and Religion

4

National elections and religious values

This essay was written in December 2004 when, by coincidence, the question of religious factors entered the field of public debate in both Australia and the United States of America.

This essay is a reflection on the political system in Australia where the people went to the polls to elect a new government to hold office for the next three years. The outcome of the election evoked strong emotional responses and considerable soul searching about our democratic processes, our deeply held beliefs and the arrogance of our "intellectual elite"

At the same time, a debate had occurred in the United States of America over a variety of ethical, bioethical and doctrinal issues that had emerged during the campaign for the election of the President of that nation.

Finally thoughtful commentaries appeared in leading journals on the nature of our governing institutions as they have evolved over the centuries of human history. These have focussed on the limits of political systems in the context of human rights and the common good of human society.

The Australian experience

On Saturday, 9 October 2004, the Australian people went to the polls to elect the next Parliament of Australia. The various parties and independent candidates had campaigned for six weeks to win the support of the electorate. During the last week, many opinion polls and most political commentators predicted a "cliff-hanger" result. At the end of polling, the media and its expert panels were poised to unravel the trend of voting and the likely composition of the new Parliament. In a state of high expectancy and confident of the good sense of the electorate, they were prepared for a long haul.

Within the first two hours, their expectations were shattered and the raw nerves of the "progressive analysts" led to exclamations of disbelief and a descent into "damage control". The winning party – the conservative coalition – by the proverbial mile, had romped home but only (we were told) because it had told outrageous lies and used scare tactics to distort the real issues espoused by the losing parties. But shock was succeeded by outrage when a long shot, purported to be the voice of a religious group of fanatical "right wingers", seemed to have exploited the electoral system to become the "balance of power" in the Upper House, even though it may win only one seat in the Senate. "It is wrong for a religious group to impose its own moral agenda on the people of Australia", claimed one commentator who seemed to be on the verge of tears. How could the electorate be so blind? How can we reconcile the articles of our democratic Constitution on the separation of the state from religion?

A very interesting question.

I leave the sober analysis of the outcome of the election to other commentators. Some of these have claimed that the signs of what happened were there to be read many months ago, that the election was never going to be close, that the winning conservatives were much more in tune with the concerns of the average voter. A groundswell of distaste had surfaced for the "progressive" agenda of small but highly vocal lobby groups and this had consolidated into a resolve that they shall no longer dictate public policy by the process of intimidation, by anti-discrimination legislation or by control of the media and the higher centres of learning.

But let us return to the question of religion. What constitutes a religious group? The word religion is taken to mean that among certain groups of people there is a belief in the existence of a higher being than man. This being is believed to be more intelligent and more powerful than man and the creator of all that exists. Its nature does not have a corporeal element that is subject to mortality and disintegration such as the human body and it exercises control over our human existence and over our ultimate destiny. Such a being is worthy of worship by man and of a trust in ultimate happiness in a future life, provided we conform to his commands over our behaviour in this life. Such a superior being is called GOD.

Today, particularly since the 18th century, such a belief is not shared by all human beings. But those who do believe claim that our experience of this world is best understood by the existence of such a being, that these conclusions are the foundation of natural theology. They claim that the experiential evidence is reinforced by rational reflection, particularly in the works of the great philosophers of antiquity and the medieval period of European and Middle East history.

Over the centuries of Judaeo-Christian history (about 4,000 years), there also exist records that are claimed to be of divine interventions. These constitute historical evidence concerning the origins of dogmas and religious practices, including the precepts that are enunciated for virtuous human behaviour. In human societies, these are based on the social institutions of marriage and family which is described as the basic unit of society. These claims are reinforced by modern psycho-social research. This in turn has evolved into the concept of the common good and this has underpinned the role of government in formulating national policy.

Whilst the evidence for a supreme being may be challenged by some sceptical philosophers and scientists, there are other philosophers, scientists and politicians who are convinced that a God exists from the evidence of intelligent design. The sceptics fall back on evasive explanations that fail to answer the ultimate question – who or what set everything in motion? To speak of a force or an energy, acting over unlimited time, does not explain the nature of the first impulse and merely stops short of tackling the ultimate inference. Those who make the claim that scientists will eventually resolve all the unanswered questions of our existence make their own act of faith in the power of scientism alone.

A feature writer for the Australian newspaper, Frank Devine, commented that the rage manifested by the "progressive left" was sheer hypocrisy, "since they have never felt the need to ward off the politically activist religious left". This selective manipulation of these politically active religious groups, purporting to be representative of Church teaching, is found to be more ideological than doctrinal, with an agenda in conflict with the basic religious beliefs of the Church with which they identify themselves. This is best illustrated in the current American political debates on the issues of abortion, embryonic stem cells and gay marriage.

The Family First Party – the long shot that may hold the balance of power in the new Australian Parliament – articulated a party platform on the basis of the common good, of its perception of the enduring values of marriage, the natural family and the fundamental principles articulated in the UN Declaration on Human Rights. It rejected the deification of the environment, but was concerned about national security when terrorism has become a universal threat and tyrannical governments have provoked a worldwide movement of refugees. It identified its values as being based on Christian principles but did not claim to impose a belief in the God of Christianity. It did not imply that a theocratic state best serves the interest of the common good of a nation such as Australia but it did seek answers from the political candidates on their basic principles when a moral decision is required.

As a political party, it remains to be seen how it will act in the interests of the common good. However we, the voters, know what moral order and social values it espouses and how its principles will be translated into political decisions, just as we knew the moral content of the platforms of the other political parties. And so the electorate used its democratic right to shape the incoming government, not out of ignorance or deceit, not out of the arrogant exhortations of the self-serving intellectual elite but out of their convictions of what really serves the common good of the Australian people.

The US political debate

In the United States of America, the battle over religion and politics followed a somewhat different course, particularly since the presidency of John Kennedy in the 1960s. At the time of his election, John Kennedy had claimed that the Pope would not dictate to him on the question of political decisions. In the lead up to the election in the first week of November, there had been considerable debate about how Catholics should not impose their beliefs on society and that the voters should observe the need for "the separation of church and state". In a frank and engaging manner, Archbishop Charles Chaput of Denver responded to these claims in an article that appeared in *The New York Times* on 22 October 2004:

> These are two of the emptiest slogans in current American politics, intended to discourage serious debate. No one in mainstream American politics wants a theocracy. Nor does anyone doubt the importance of morality in public life. Therefore, we should recognise these slogans for what they are: frequently dishonest and ultimately dangerous sound bites.

> Lawmaking inevitably involves some group imposing its beliefs on the rest of us. That's the nature of the democratic process. If we say that we "ought" to do something, we are making a moral judgment. When our legislators turn that judgment into law, somebody's ought becomes a "must" for the whole of society. This is not inherently dangerous; it's how pluralism works.

> Democracy depends on people of conviction expressing

their views, confidently and without embarrassment. This give-and-take is an American tradition, and religious believers play a vital role in it. We don't serve our country – in fact we weaken it intellectually – if we downplay our principles or fail to speak forcefully out of some misguided sense of good manners.

People who support permissive abortion laws have no qualms about imposing their views on society. Often working against popular opinion, they have tried to block any effort to change permissive abortion laws since the Supreme Court's *Roe v Wade* decision in 1973. That's fair. That's their right. But why should the rules of engagement be different for citizens who oppose those laws?

Catholics have an obligation to work for the common good and the dignity of every person. We see abortion as a matter of civil rights and human dignity, not simply as a matter of religious teaching. We are doubly unfaithful – both to our religious convictions and to our democratic responsibilities – if we fail to support the right to life of the unborn child. Our duties to social justice by no means end there. But they do always begin there, because the right to life is foundational.

For Catholics to take a "pro-choice" view toward abortion contradicts our identity and makes us complicit in how the choice plays out. The "choice" in abortion always involves the choice to end the life of an unborn human being. For anyone who sees this fact clearly, neutrality, silence or private disapproval are not options. They are evils almost as grave as abortion itself. If religious believers do not advance their convictions about public morality in public debate, they are demonstrating not tolerance but cowardice.

The civil order has its own sphere of responsibility, and its own proper autonomy, apart from the church or any other religious community. But civil authorities are never exempt from moral engagement and criticism, either from the Church or its members. The founders themselves realised this.

The founders sought to prevent the establishment of an official state church. Given America's history of anti-Catholic nativism, Catholics strongly support the Constitution's approach to religious freedom. But the Constitution does not, nor was it ever intended to, prohibit people or communities of faith from playing an active role in public life. Exiling religion from civic debate separates government from morality and citizens from their consciences. That road leads to politics without character, now a national epidemic.

Words are cheap. Actions matter. If we believe in the sanctity of life from conception to natural death, we need to prove that by our actions, including our political choices. Anything less leads to the corruption of our integrity. Patriotism, which is a virtue for people of all faiths, requires that we fight, ethically and non-violently, for what we believe.

Claiming that "we don't want to impose our beliefs on

society" is not merely politically convenient; it is morally incoherent and irresponsible.

As James 2:17 reminds us, in a passage quoted in the final presidential debate, "Faith without works is dead." It is a valid point. People should act on what they claim to believe. Otherwise they are violating their own conscience, and lying to themselves and the rest of us.

The nature of governments

In *Crisis* magazine (October 2004), B.J. Wiker, a senior Fellow at the Discovery Institute, wrote an article entitled "Why You Must Vote in the November Elections in the USA". Wiker claims that we cannot look to politics as the pathway to the salvation of the human race but we can, at least in a democracy, use our vote to elect politicians of integrity who espouse the values that will contribute to the common good of a society that seeks the truth about human existence.

He then discusses the works of Aristotle who described democracy as the best of the worst forms of government. According to Aristotle, "There are six forms of government, three good and three bad. To list them in order from best to worst: the three good regimes are Kingship, Aristocracy and Polity. The three bad regimes are Democracy, Oligarchy and Tyranny. What divides the good from the bad is simply this. The good regimes whether they are ruled by one person (kingship), a few (aristocracy), or the majority (polity), are ruled in accordance with the true good of human nature and for the benefit of everybody (the ruled as well as the rulers). The bad regimes – whether they are ruled by the majority (democracy), by the few (oligarchy), or by one (tyranny) – are not directed to the true good but to the private gratifications of the passions of the rulers."

Aristotle, however, was aware that human beings are prone to wickedness and corruption and therefore are likely to adopt bad forms of government. There is fine line between kingship and tyranny, between aristocracy and oligarchy. The least dangerous is democracy but this too can be corrupted and eroded by the social values that it embraces. Wiker observes that the American Constitution was built upon shared pre-political moral truths, enunciated over the centuries by the Judeo-Christian tradition and these truths were not democratically derived. Their source was of divine origin – the kingdom of God.

With the emergence of secularism and the secular state, Western democracy was infected with a political virus that has now emerged as the postmodern state. The underlying philosophy of this "school of thought" is scrambled and incoherent but at the level of social values, it rests on the language of relativism. Relativism is the new religion and its proponents are dogmatic in their passionate expressions of their beliefs and their demands.

The new player in the field of politics is Islamic fundamentalism, based on a tyranny of a theocratic regime supported globally by the concept of the jihad or "holy war".

In this confusion of political forces, there is a pluralism of social philosophies, a plethora of political parties and strident lobby groups, so that democracy needs to steer a chartered course. Wiker describes what he calls an extreme democracy where "the passion for equality is all-consuming, spreading to every aspect of life, so that not only are all citizens treated equally under the law but all opinions, all passions, all views of what is good are treated as equally meritorious". The moral and social outcomes for the philosophy of relativism and the political outcomes of secularism are now glaringly apparent and the electorates in Australia and the United States of America have been aroused.

A new chartered course

To find a new charter in the field of democratic politics, it is obvious that all voices must be heard. The philosophical sceptics postulate that religious beliefs on the existence of God are irrational and unscientific and therefore should be laughed out of the court of public consideration. "Not so," says John Haldane, an English philosopher, in his recent book: *An Intelligent Person's Guide to Religion*. The claim of the sceptics is bogus. Religious beliefs, especially in the monotheistic religions, have at least an equal footing in rational thought and apologetics as do the arguments of atheists or agnostics. Haldane states (page 70):

> In the face of the anti-religious triumphalism of Dawkins and the marginally lesser presumption of Wilson, I have argued that there is life in the old arguments for the existence of God. I have also indicated how believers may equip themselves to defend their faith on the basis of reasoning that has the power to elicit respect from the genuinely scientifically minded. If I am correct, then the achievement of philosophical theology in establishing the existence of God explains both why science can work, and why some of science's achievements are bad. The first

because the world has an intelligible order to which science can conform itself; the second because there is also a moral order which the use of these scientific achievements may violate. Neither fact is something that science itself can explain. Yet both are explained on the assumption that the world is the product of intelligent design.

The state cannot, without adopting a tyrannical or totalitarian regime, exclude consideration of the arguments of those who believe in the common good as derived from a belief in an ultimate supreme being. The state itself cannot adopt a specific religious denomination as a state religion but there are many human values that are shared across the diversity of religious beliefs and by those who profess no belief in a deity. These are the pre-political values mentioned by Wiker. In a democracy, all have a voice and all eligible adults have a right to vote for a candidate of their choice. Equally, the electorate has a right to know the basic ideology or social philosophy of the candidates and the political parties, to determine their understanding of the common good of the community. This will be reflected in their answers to questions on vital ethical and moral issues that impinge on the decisions of the electorate.

That is why Archbishop Chaput is right when he says that the rules of engagement apply equally to both sides of the debate on religion and politics. In politics, a great deal of legislation involves moral decisions, how we should act on a particular issue. Archbishop Chaput draws attention to this reality and challenges those who do not believe in God to justify their own basic beliefs and ethical standards as best serving the common good of human society. The same applies to both sides of the debate. For the community to decide, both sides must be allowed equal opportunities to enter the public square so that the impact of political proposals can be measured by the electorate.

5

The family and the political system

This paper was originally presented at the Sorrento, Victoria,
meeting of Catenians on 13 August 2010.

I was reading recently a small book with the intriguing title *Me and My Dad*, compiled and illustrated by Stuart Hample. It contained a series of short opinion pieces articulated by children between the ages of seven and 11. One quote caught my eye and stirred my musing soul: "Even if I'm bad, my Dad has to still like me because I am in his family. I think it's a law." *Alison.*

I set the book aside, sat down and pondered. This comment is an interesting one for it is an extension of what we ascribe to the individual person. It refers to the social character of our human existence, to the fact that we are social beings, living in communities with basic units of social identity, of social nurture and social integration, extending into a concept of the common good of communities of people which should be the core principle of a democratic political system.

In the context of a human individual, a law means an established order or system built into the very nature of someone who happens to be a member of the human species. We are talking about the human species and not about other forms of living creatures; about our rights, our duties and responsibilities towards each other. It is what we mean by the term, "the natural law", what is imprinted into the very structure of our human constitution or nature. But how do we know about this law, even as a child?

Fundamentally we know it from two sources – from simple observation (empirical evidence) and logical analysis over time, and from divine revelation. It is moulded into our very being and shapes us as individual human persons with profound social dimensions.

We observe that as human beings, there are two genders, two sexes that are physically, sexually and psychologically complementary; who join in sexual unions that are potentially fruitful; who bear a new generation of human beings who recognise that they have progenitors (their parents); a mother and a father, biologically and psychologically bonded into what we recognise and call the "natural family". Even a child can recognise and accept this intimate relationship that binds together its constituent members. This is how the family emerged from the complementarity of the sexes.

In the documents that we have received in the Old and New Testaments (the Christian Bible which Chrisitians accept as divine revelation), we note in the Pentateuch, the first five books of the Old Testament, how the Judeo-Christian concept of marriage between a man and a woman was established from the beginning of human creation.

The fundamental structure of marriage as a lifelong, exclusive union between a man and a woman was reiterated by Christ in his famous comment to the apostles that "in the beginning it was not so"; it was not meant to be a breakable institution, nor a union determined by so-called sexual orientation. It is a freely entered contract between a man and a woman (UN Declaration of Human Rights).

In more recent times, the anthropologist George Murdock, in a cross cultural study found that the institution of marriage existed in every known human society and he outlined the four functions and features that existed in all nuclear families – the sexual, the economic, the reproductive and the educational. He went on to say, "The immense social utility of the nuclear family and the basic reason for its universality thus begin to emerge in strong relief."

In other words, the institutions of marriage and family predated the establishment of the state with its legislative powers. However what predated the state was the recognition that certain norms were established within the clan or tribe that were a feature of the basic unit of social development as the nuclear family extended its relationships across the generations of its members.

In fact the family and not the individual is the basic unit of social living which is another feature of our human nature. As individuals we live in relationships to others and this has been articulated in the two great commandments of love – to love God and to love our neighbour.

As I was researching many sources for this paper, I came across an interesting article in my archives. It was written by the great Catholic historian of the last century – Christopher Dawson. It was published in 1933 and traced the development of the family before the period of Jewish history and of classical Greece; and it explained the dramatic effect on Roman and European culture that occurred with the growth of Christendom after Pentecost. I do not have the time to dwell on this outstanding and prescient essay but I wish to take you forward into the modern era that followed the Second World War. (Christopher Dawson, *Dynamics of World History*, "The Patriarchal Family in History", pp. 165-174.)

Nor do I have the time to discuss the encyclical *Humanae Vitae*, promulgated by Pope Paul VI in 1968 and in which he set out the norms of a valid marriage. They are conjugal love, conjugal fidelity, responsibility for parenthood, responsible parenthood and a sacramental form of public announcement and celebration. I encourage you to read again this encyclical and to ponder on each one of these norms and their internal interplay.

About 25 years ago, I gave a talk at Camberwell to a parents' group. The subject that I chose was "The Domestic Church". This is an extract from that lecture:

> The (Catholic) family is the smallest unit of a community of believers in our Lord and God, Jesus Christ. It is a close-knit community which mirrors the union between Christ and his Church and is centred on love and life. It is based on the marks of marriage between a man and a woman which is exclusive and faithful and fruitful. They share a common belief in Christ and his teaching Church. They grow in number by the birth of their children who are also instructed in the faith and through their shared beliefs and practices form the fundamental units of the wider ecclesia.

> It is within the family that the faith is nurtured and deepened in its understanding of God's revelation. But the nurturing of the faith demands an active effort on the part of parents who have the obligation to impart the truths revealed by

God and by the Church which He empowered to teach in his name.

This type of instruction is a continuing one and needs to be reinforced by the worship of God, by prayer and the regular use of the sources of grace to be found in the sacraments and the performance of charitable works.

The family is the ideal setting for the development of these beliefs and virtues because it is the most profound medium for the transmission of true love and the respect of every human individual. The members of the family are in constant communion with each other. They share the deepest intimacies and confidences. They support each other as no other grouping of people can do. They have the power to enrich their faith and to evangelise the wider community.

Today I would add a further dimension to this description, one articulated by Peter and Brigette Berger, outstanding sociologists of very recent times. They speak of the family as a foundational "mediating structure" wherein one generation of progenitors nurture and introduce the next generation into the wider society, having shaped their behaviour and their particular moral code: to meet the challenges and demands that they will encounter as individuals in a very diversified world of opportunities and personal responsibilities.

Today that is a very secular and materially orientated world, sparkling with irreligious attractions and images and lifestyles. It is a world of economic instability and aggressive assaults on religious institutions and social constructs such as marriage and family which have evolved over many centuries of social development. The predominant philosophy is personal autonomy and moral relativism.

It is a world of sexual licence and sexual predation, of pornography and sexual imagery masquerading as advertisements. It is a world of celebrities promoted as models, of household formations that exclude reproductive responsibility, where interest in children is often awakened late in the fertile lifespan of the many women who are then attracted to modern reproductive technology, a growth industry of the modern era. It is a period of great global mobility, of tourism, of mass movements of oppressed people, of the collapse of European Christendom and the opening up of Eastern nations and cultures. It is a time when the growth centres of Catholicism are in Africa and Asia whilst Western Catholicism languishes from population decline and the scandals of clerical sexual abuse and the plunge in the image of episcopal authority.

But simultaneously there has been a great resurgence in the enthusiasm of the crowds that attend World Youth Day, the demonstrations in support of traditional marriage and the family, the protection of human life in the womb. These have occurred around the world, not only in Africa and Asia but also in Europe. So we need to capture the moment, even though there have been some strange responses coming from American Catholic universities and from many elected politicians who parade their "Catholicity".

Conclusion

In the context of this reflection and complementary to my talk in September last year (2009) in Bacchus Marsh, I would suggest that

Catenians who are parents, at a time when elections are being held for our Federal and State parliaments, might give consideration to two pieces of advice that had been canvassed from me over the last few months.

1. Normative Education.

Normative education is concerned with inculcating patterns of ethical behaviour, particularly in the formative years of childhood development. A child learns the norms of human behaviour within a variety of social settings – the home and family, the neighbourhood environment, the school and other educational institutions, at work and at play, in all relationships that develop during his or her lifetime. These norms are based on a system of moral values that shape his or her personality and social identity, and which underlie every decision that he or she has to make at every level of daily living.

The values that a person acquires depend on an appreciation of the way we should act towards other people and on the religious beliefs (or lack of them) that we embrace as guidelines for our social behaviour and interior faith.

These norms of behaviour are transmitted in a variety of ways but the most important is the witness given by parents and other persons who figure prominently in the daily life of a person. This is a process of modelling which is reinforced with verbal communication between next of kin and other recognised educators. It is demonstrated in the way we as parents live our own lives, in our practice of the faith, in attendance at Mass and the sacraments, in our prayer life, and our daily tasks.

It can be a daunting task but it is rewarded richly by the one who has sent us.

2. To a Christian Politician (July 2010)

On the question of religious beliefs and a political career, it seems to me that one should declare what motivates your everyday actions. One should be able to say that you are a practising Christian who agrees with the International Instruments that Australia has ratified, particularly with those that acknowledge *inalienable* individual rights, and those that pertain to the family as the basic unit of society and to the principles of the Convention on the Rights of the Child. In a multicultural society as exists in Australia, there is no place for a theocratic or totalitarian ruling class but there is a place for the public articulation of basic beliefs and the opportunity to debate them publicly without venom or perversion by friend or foe. That is a complex phenomenon that requires patient and careful articulation, best done in a well presented essay that irons out the various disputable issues that currently cloud the public square.

At the moment, the public square is dominated by the mainstream media with an infinite capacity to use rhetorical statements and assertive language as if no argument exists, other than their own stated viewpoints. Across a broad spectrum of political and scientific endeavour, ideology reigns supreme, aided and abetted by deep vested interests and academic forces that follow a pathway of moral relativism.

6

Reason and faith
in the new millennium

Towards the end of 2006, Pope Benedict XVI delivered several addresses to bishops making their *ad limina* visits to the Vatican, especially to the Swiss and German delegations. His comments ranged over such issues as the sanctity of human life, modern reproductive technology especially the destruction of human embryos for "altruistic" purposes, marriage and the family, and the hierarchy of human values. In his weekly comment, Sandro Magister, a Catholic journalist and Vatican watcher, wrote as follows:

> Benedict replied to what is, perhaps, the objection most commonly directed against the Pope and the Church hierarchy by progressive Catholic circles. The objection is that, in the cases of life and the family, the Church's hierarchy preaches truths defined as non-negotiable, pure and solid, binding even in political decisions, while in the areas of peace, justice, and the protection of the environment, it waters down "Christian distinctiveness" and makes feeble statements, acquiescing to the temporal powers. According to the progressive Catholic circles, the priority should be reversed. The Church should put in the

first place the struggle for peace, justice, and the defence of nature, and should be more understanding towards modern "subjectivity" in the areas of life and the family.

That is quite a mouthful. The propositions in this presentation by Magister all claim to be moral values that are challenged in our everyday lives. At first sight, we are conscious that peace, justice, the care of nature, concern about suffering, all carry moral overtones. Christ himself addressed many of these issues in the beatitudes and in his parables and the Church has frequently spoken about them in public statements. But the manner in which these matters are addressed can be seductive and misleading when one realises that Christ commissioned his Church to teach all that He himself had taught his apostles and disciples.

It is interesting to read what Pope Benedict XVI said about these dilemmas. His reply is to be found in the homily he gave at the second meeting with the Swiss bishops on 9 November 2006. At this meeting, the Pope did not have a prepared text but he spoke extemporaneously, off the cuff, with great clarity. The first part of his talk was devoted to prayer, how to communicate and listen to God, with references to Augustine, Aquinas and Ignatius, even when God seems to be silent. Then he launched into the second part of his discussion on morals and I reproduce this section in full, from the *L'Osservatore Romano*.

The second thing that I have remembered in these very days concerns morals. I often hear it said that people today have a longing for God, for spirituality, for religion, and are starting once again to see the Church as a possible conversation partner from which, in this regard, they can receive something.

Awareness is growing: the Church especially conveys spiritual experience; she is like a tree where the birds can make their nests even if they want to fly away again later – but she is precisely also a place where one can settle for a certain time. Instead, what people find more difficult is the morality that the Church proclaims. I have pondered on this – I have been pondering on it for a long time – and I see ever more clearly that in our age morality is, as it were, split in two.

Modern society not only merely lacks morals but has "discovered" and demands another dimension of morality, which in the Church's proclamation in recent decades and even earlier perhaps, has not been sufficiently presented. This dimension includes the great topics of peace, non-violence, justice for all, concern for the poor and respect for creation. They have become an ethical whole which, precisely as a political force, has great power and for many constitutes the substitution or succession of religion. Instead of religion, seen as metaphysical and as something from above – perhaps also as something individualistic – the great moral themes come into play as the essential which then confers dignity on man and engages him.

This is one aspect: this morality exists and it also fascinates young people, who work for peace, for non-violence, for justice, for the poor, for creation. And there are truly great moral themes that also belong, moreover, to the tradition of the Church. The means offered for their solution, however, are often very unilateral and not always credible, but we cannot dwell on this now. The important topics are present.

The other part of morality, often received controversially by politics, concerns life. One aspect of it is the commitment to life from conception to death, that is, its defence against abortion, against euthanasia, against the manipulation and man's self-authorisation in order to dispose of life. People often seek to justify these interventions with the seemingly great purpose of thereby serving the future generations, and it even appears moral to take human life into one's own hands and manipulate it.

However, on the other hand, the knowledge also exists that human life is a gift that demands our respect and love from the very first to its very last moments, also for the suffering, the disabled and the weak.

The morality of marriage and the family also fits into this context. Marriage is becoming, so to speak, ever more marginalised. We are aware of the example of certain countries where legislation has been modified so that marriage is no longer defined as a bond between a man and a woman but a bond between persons; with this, obviously, the basic idea is destroyed and society from its roots becomes something quite different.

The awareness that sexuality, eros and marriage as a union between a man and a woman go together – "and they become one flesh" (Gn 2:24) – this knowledge is growing weaker and weaker; every type of bond seems entirely normal – they represent a sort of overall morality of non-discrimination and a form of freedom due to man. Naturally, with this the indissolubility of marriage has become almost a utopian idea which many public figures seem precisely to contradict. So it is that even the family is gradually breaking up.

There are of course many explanations for the problem of the sharp decline in the birth rate, but certainly a decisive role is also played in this by the fact that people want to enjoy life, that they have little confidence in the future and that they feel the family is no longer viable as a lasting community in which future generations may grow up.

In these contexts, therefore, our proclamation clashes with an awareness, as it were, contrary to society and with a sort of anti-morality based on a conception of freedom seen as the faculty to choose autonomously with no predefined guidelines, as non-discrimination, hence, as the approval of every type of possibility. Thus, it autonomously establishes itself as ethically correct, but the other awareness has not disappeared. It exists, and I believe we must commit ourselves to reconnecting these two parts of morality and to making it clear that they must be inseparably united.

Only if human life from conception until death is respected is the ethic of peace possible and credible; only then may non-violence be expressed in every direction, only then can we truly accept creation and only then can we achieve true justice.

I think that this is the great task we have before us: on the one hand, not to make Christianity seem merely morality, but rather a gift in which we are given the love that sustains us and provides us with the strength we need to be able to "lose our own life". On the other hand, in this context of freely given love, we need to move forward towards ways of putting it into practice, whose foundation is always offered to us by the decalogue, which we must interpret today with Christ and with the Church in a progressive and new way.

Commentary (JNS)

To return to what Benedict XVI said, "We must commit ourselves to reconnecting these two parts of morality and to making it clear that they must be inseparably united ... Only if human life from conception until death is respected is the ethic of peace possible and credible – only then may non-violence be expressed ... Only then can we achieve true justice."

The Pope alludes to matters that are metaphysical, that originate from above our material experiences, that are difficult to understand but which are in accord with the nature of all that God has created. Some of these questions relate to experiences that may distress us, such as suffering, poverty, inequality, violent behaviour, greed and the struggle for power over others. These rightly distress us but can lead to a diversion of our attention from the full panorama of divine revelation. The danger arises that we can distort the moral order of divine revelation, even to the point of failing to listen to vital teachings.

On the day after his meeting with the Swiss bishops, the Pope also met with a delegation of bishops from Germany and this time he had a prepared document. Before reading this address, we need to remember that in the history of mankind, the moral law has passed through three periods of development. From the time of Adam and Eve, man first abided by his intuitive knowledge of the Natural Law and his conversations with God. When Adam and Eve disobeyed, original sin entered the world. Man became subject to sin and then occurred the second phase of moral development – the Decalogue or the Mosaic Law. Finally we entered the third phase with the advent of Christ who came not to destroy the Law but to fulfil it and to perfect it. Across the history of mankind, these three elements of the moral law have coalesced to shape our understanding of our relationship to God and our pathway to holiness.

In his address to the German bishops, the Pope drew attention to the secularisation of the Western world and to the encounter between secular values and Christian values. Even as we dialogue with the secular world, and for that matter also with the Muslim world, Christians should enter the engagement with a spirit of hope and conviction in the arguments that they can advance in the defence of their faith. He particularly laid emphasis on religious education in the schools, the imparting of sound doctrine based on the *Catechism of the Catholic Church*, the training of religious teachers who are models of practising Catholics, and schools that are imbued with a Catholic ethos. He drew attention to the duty of bishops to ensure that the religious curricula were soundly based and properly imparted and that this ethos should be visible in the role of pastoral workers who work closely with the priests who have been properly formed in the seminaries and theological faculties.

What has not been adequately addressed in this question of dialogue is the corruption of words and the secular flight from reason. Of particular interest is the use of words like justice, rights, compassion, altruism, peace, truth and discrimination. A lot more needs to be said about the concept of the common good, about rational debate and about scientific integrity. The arguments for a supreme being need to be re-articulated and the evidence for a divine revelation should be taught with sound reasoning.

Pope Benedict XVI has now on many occasions called for rational discourse on any subject that engages the mind of human beings. In particular, he has commented on the need to recognise that in the field of morality there exists a hierarchy of values that should operate in any human society, that without a right to life there can be no true justice, without a proper concept of marriage there can be no family structure that perpetuates the human race and protects the upbringing of new generations and trust between spouses, that without honesty and integrity there can be no true justice, that compassion can be a distortion of justice, and that science cannot be the arbiter of ethical behaviour.

The Pope's addresses to the Swiss and German delegations of bishops were a challenge to the Catholic world of today. His remarks were not meant to be a series of rebukes to Church leaders and wayward groups in the ranks of the clergy and the laity. He was analysing the crisis of Christian belief and practice in the modern Western world. In other discourses he has pointed to the impressive growth of the Catholic Church in the Third World, especially in Africa and Asia. He has spoken with great learning, with a sense of deep faith in the risen Christ. He has appealed to the use of reason and for a growth in our knowledge of the history of the Church and its saints and for a return to a prayerful relationship to God. He has applauded the Church's involvement in charitable works and services and in the evolution of the institutions of learning. His call to the bishops of some European nations was to awaken the need to acquire a mature and accurate knowledge of the Catholic faith, to experience its spiritual dimensions and to understand the importance of being a witness to the full message of that living faith.

The task facing the Western world is monumental. Many of its leaders are hostile to the morality articulated by Christ and the Church that He founded. The academic world, the world of art and fashion, the world of advertising and sensational journalism, all are pervaded by the philosophy of the post-modern era which rejects objective morality and is preoccupied by autonomous rights and a belief in the exercise of a rampant and undisciplined conscience.

The prevailing philosophy is known as relativism which is subjectively driven and is the focus of many articles by Pope Benedict XVI. In an introduction to a recent book, entitled *In the Light of Christ: Writings in the Western Tradition*, Lucy Becket describes relativism in the following way:

> In the intellectual climate of the liberal West in our time, the very words "truth," "beauty" and "goodness", cannot be used without embarrassment except in relation not to God but to the individual, who, in a biological accident in a random universe, chooses what seems, for the moment, to be true or good or beautiful to himself. That individual may defend such choices, but on personal, subjective grounds

only; the one remaining moral imperative commanding general assent is that the choices of others must have equal status to one's own and should not be regarded as bad unless they do harm to others, measurable in a utilitarian fashion. Anyone may try to persuade others that his view, his perspective, is "better" than theirs, but this effort will be no more than a game, a power game, played in emptiness. Nietzsche, who presides over the contemporary academy, towards the end of the 19th century called "perspective" the basic condition of all life and the "will to power" the basic drive of the human world ... The only intellectual consensus is that there is no consensus.

The English philosopher Roger Scruton is a forthright critic of this Western liberal school of contemporary academia. In an interesting article published in 1999, he gave it the title "What Ever Happened to Reason?" After demonstrating the flight from rational debate by the post-modern philosophers, he observes that our current problem is that the arguments for a traditional, objective morality do not appeal to the modern gurus of Western academia and a large population of Western society has lost interest in listening to the voice of reason.

I am not sure that this is true, even for the societies that grew out of the cultures of Greece, Rome and the spread of Christianity. There is evidence that the majority of people live and want to live within a natural family structure and that they recognise the features of good parenting and the level of social dysfunction that results from the breakdown of the natural family. There is evidence of a sense of social repugnance to the betrayal of the marriage vows and the claim of same sex relationships as being equivalent to the relationships within the traditional family. The falling birth rate, the inversion of the population pyramid with its base moving to the top and threatening the national economy, the awareness of the psychological and physical trauma caused by induced abortion, the mounting suspicion of the motives of many scientists in the field of reproductive technology and the challenge to promiscuous sexual behaviour by religious forces in the community, all point to a growing awareness that the common good is not served well by the philosophy of relativism.

There is also evidence that there are major problems with our use of slogans and even words when put in conjunction. Peace does not necessarily lead to justice and freedom to choose (as occurred at Yalta in 1945, in Vietnam in 1975 and Munich in 1938); justice can be corrupted by the claims of bogus "rights" and self-interest; compassion can lead to injustice (the embryo legislation), and the unravelling of the DNA molecule and the human genome has thrown doubts on the hypothesis of random selection in evolutionary theory. The youth of today is showing renewed interest in a divine creator and many are rejecting the values espoused by the youth of yesteryear. This is all happening within the Western culture whilst in the East and many countries of the Third World, Christianity is gaining strength.

Then I read Pope Benedict XVI's homily to the Swiss bishops on 7 November, given during the course of the votive Mass (*L'Osservatore Romano*, 22 November 2006). It is well worth reading. After quoting from Gregory the Great, Benedict asks the question: What should we do? His reply is not only illuminating but thought provoking.

I hold that the first thing to do is ... what St. Paul cries to us in God's Name: "Your attitude must be Christ's." Learn to think as Christ thought, learn to think with Him! And this thinking is not only the thinking of the mind, but also a thinking of the heart.

It is in this way that we capture the joy of God's word in our hearts and in our minds, that "we know him in the face of Jesus Christ who suffered for us". What the Pope is saying is that we need to turn our attention to the redemptive love of Christ, that He moves into centre stage, that our focus shifts from ourselves to a divine revelation in the person of Christ. We need to know him from the evidence of his existence on earth, from the gospel accounts of his life, of his sayings and of his deeds. We need to become aware that He speaks with the authority of God himself, that his passion and death reveal the depth of divine redemptive love. By bringing Christ into the centre of our thoughts, we begin to understand that there is a being who is concerned about us and the way we should behave towards one another and towards the one who created us.

We learn these things through apologetics, through the deposit of faith that Christ revealed and confirmed, and which He empowered his Church to teach with authority. But He gave us more than this. He instituted the sacraments as sources of grace and the Mass, with its liturgy and its universality. There is a dimension to our lives that internalises the unique relationship that we have to God, that deepens our appreciation of his nature and holiness, in which we can share. It imparts to us an *ethos* that embraces not only our personal selves but also the community of people who share in these experiences. It moves beyond mere reasonable argument and scholarship, that is, beyond the powers of the mind, to the very core of our being, to what we call the heart of man, to an understanding of what we mean by faith. We enter the world of prayer, the joy of songs in praise of the Lord, to a sense of peace in our souls. Liturgy is an important component of our lives for it elevates our thoughts and our attention to meditation on the ultimate meaning of our lives and redemptive grace – its metaphysical dimension.

This ethos permeated our churches and our institutions, and motivated the educators of our children, parents and teachers alike. But we are now in a cycle of profound change where the new ethos is established by non-spiritual sources and by enemies both within and outside the Church. Within our Western culture, the outcome has been catastrophic. It seems that the work of Christ has failed and his message is widely rejected. But the Pope speaks in more hopeful tones for this has happened before. Christ has always found the answer to those who seem to reject him. He moves slowly in our time frame but those who remain faithful to his call can share in our ultimate revival. The Pope is not only appealing to bishops and religious bodies but to the whole of the Church to once again become living witnesses to his divine love.

The more that any society operates under these values, the more does that society achieve true peace; with respect for human life and concern for our neighbour, the more can be achieved to relieve suffering and to protect and care for the disabled; the more that we honour the virtue of justice, the less will discrimination be tolerated. As the Pope has said, it can only come from the top down – a vertical transmission to be spread horizontally.

SECTION 3

Theology and the Catholic layman

7

"I am the Way, the Truth and the Life"

The following reflection was presented during the Holy Hour Celebration at Our Lady of Perpetual Help Catholic Church in Dromana, Victoria, on Sunday, 16 October 2005, to mark the closing of the Year on the Eucharist.

The Holy Eucharist was instituted by Christ on the night before his passion and death. At the same time, He instituted the ministerial priesthood, those members of his Church empowered by the Holy Spirit to change bread and wine into his body and blood as a commemoration of him and his passion and death. From the very beginning of the Church, the Eucharist was the great mystery that was universally accepted by the Christian community. It is referred to in the New Testament, especially in the writings of St. Paul, and later in the many documents of the earliest fathers of the Church. It was central to the liturgy of the Church and formed the canon of the Mass throughout Christendom.

It was defined as an article of the Catholic faith by the Council of Trent in the 16th century, after Christendom split into dissident factions. It has been celebrated over the past year at a time when Christianity is under a monstrous assault by the forces of secular humanism and other militant groups.

During his final discourse to the apostles at the Last Supper, Thomas asked Christ to tell us the way to the Father.

"Have you not known me," Christ replied.

"I am the way, the truth and the life."

It is that short sentence that I have taken as the basis of this meditation today.

The Truth

According to St. Thomas Aquinas, truth is synonymous with being, with existing. But when Christ says that He is the truth, He is referring to ultimate truth upon which depend all other things that exist. He is claiming to be God. He is eternal in his existence. He has always been and will always be. He identifies himself as the Son of God, the second person of the Holy Trinity. Within the mystery of the Trinity, the Father is within him and He is in the Father in communion with the Holy Spirit who proceeds from the Father and the Son.

He is describing the great mystery of the Holy Trinity, the existence of a personalised God consisting of three divine persons whose existence is not like ours. He is a pure spirit, a concept that is difficult for our minds to grasp but we can know of his existence through his works and his attributes. And we come to acknowledge his dominion over us through the gift of faith.

Christ then elaborates on the great mystery of his incarnation.

He has been sent by the Father to redeem mankind, to forgive our sins so that we can be reconciled with the Father but this can only be achieved by the supreme act of sacrificing his physical life to restore the original friendship that existed between created man and the Creator. He claimed to be the son of man, born of a woman, true God and true man and only through him can we come to the Father. St. John the Baptist identified him as the Lamb of God, the One Who would be sacrificed to redeem mankind.

The Way

Therefore He is the way, the anointed one – the highway to the triune God. It is a highway of life built on the two great commandments of love. By his death on the cross, He revealed the depth of his love for us. But He also said: "If you love me, you will keep my commandments." This is part of the truth, the reality that exists, because it has been revealed by him, the source of all that exists. His mission is not only the redemption of mankind but to set the pattern of how we should live our lives in accordance with the commandments enunciated by him.

The Life

But Christ is also the life and now we move into the next great mystery of our existence – God's reason for creating us. We enter into the mystery of divine life, into the mystery of grace for which we can find no easy expression due to the limitation of our human experience in this world. We try to explain what it is by analogy or by parables. But it is obvious that the experience of divine life is offered to us as a gift that is gratuitous, a gift that our human nature does not deserve and which surpasses all our expectations of living as human beings. By the gift of grace, we are called to be more than what we are as mere human beings.

We are to become adopted children of God and are offered the eternal joy and peace of holiness, as God is holy. After we pass into the next world, we will come to understand the nature of divine love which pervades the relationship between the three divine persons. That is why grace is described as sanctifying, a gift that draws us into the bosom of all that is holy, the state of ultimate happiness.

The Eucharist

And how do we strive towards this end? "Unless you eat my flesh and drink my blood, you will have no life in you." So, on the night before Christ died, He instituted the sacrament of the Eucharist so that He could enter into a divine and most intimate communion with us in this life and be forever present in our midst as we stumble on the highway to the promised land.

These are the thoughts that we should meditate on and try to plumb the depths of human understanding and appreciation. Our faith in Christ that He is who He claims to be will convince us of the ultimate truth. Hope will spur us on to seek the gift of eternal life that we can enjoy only in part in this life through the gift of sanctifying grace. But charity – the love of God and neighbour, the two great commandments of love – enables us in this life to see through the glass darkly and to gain some awareness of the splendour and glory of divine love and holiness found in the Trinity.

St. Thomas Aquinas wrote the hymns in praise of this great sacrament. We too can add our own silent prayers of veneration as we contemplate the wonder of the real presence of God in our midst.

In a letter to the Romans (6.22-27), St. Paul says that we are not to worry if we cannot choose the right words to pray as we would wish. The Holy Spirit will transmit the thoughts that enter our hearts, for He knows perfectly well what we are trying to express through the process of meditating on the truth of our existence and the truth of the holiness of the three persons of the Trinity.

8

Musings on the Godhead

Preamble

This short reflection is a brief summary of a train of thought stretching over a long period of time. It has involved many scattered ideas that I wrote into diaries of sorts as I attended conferences around the world before I attempted to draw them together. They grew out of a dialogue with others, and were enhanced by many lecturers who were great teachers and patient listeners; but in the end they would reveal what St. Augustine discovered many centuries ago – beyond a certain point of human reason we cannot go, for we do not possess all the knowledge that resides in the mind of a transcendent God. But belief in the evidence that we do have brings us closer to the divine essence. Our best evidence lies in the historical figure of Jesus Christ. I believe from the evidence that He is the person who He claimed to be.

* * *

I was initially struck by a passage from the writings of St. Augustine: "I believe so that I may understand."

This saying needs to be understood in both scientific and philosophical-theological terms. Over the years, I have read a great deal in several fields of human endeavour. In some I have studied to gain professional qualifications whilst in others I have pursued peripheral interests as the outcome of my involvement with non-government organisations in the general community.

My chosen professional career has been in the field of medicine, medical research including epidemiology and medical ethics, where researchers observe the world around us. As a human being, living in a material universe, I seek explanations for objective findings about the universe – the empirical evidence. I observe that there are laws that govern the non-living and living components of a system that I perceive through my five human senses – touch, sight, hearing, smell and taste. The senses send information into a human faculty known as the intellect, which processes and analyses the information and then explores the possible causes of why things are what we find them to be. This searching by the intellect to advance on the empirical knowledge that we acquire from scientific studies leads to the field of natural theology.

In doing so, through the use of reason, I have come to the belief that I cannot summarily dismiss the possibility that there is a God, a supreme (divine) being who is the creator of all material things and beings in existence. If I reject *a priori* the possibility of such a God Who can create something material from a non-material source, then I am wilfully excluding a major possible explanation of the origin of all matter in the universe. In other words, I am seeking the ultimate cause of everything in existence. Moreover I find that the scientific method must harness the power of reason and the use of the intellect in order to find the ultimate first cause of the material universe and an understanding of the concept of human dignity which has been conferred on the species *homo sapiens.*

I believe that there is evidence of an intelligent designer of the universe, both from a philosophical point of view and from empirical evidence-based on scientific studies of the world around us and particularly in the biological sciences.

In the field of science, the scientific method is based on probabilities that an hypothesis is true but is ultimately unable to pronounce that the ultimate truth has been exposed and entirely understood.

The question of a spiritual being called God is posed by the discipline of historiography, the system of discovering, verifying and recording past events and of analysing them for posterity. The history of a divine being who is the first cause of everything extends back to our earliest records of human life and human activity but there is one fundamental doctrine that attempts to analyse the very nature of God who, I believe, is the ultimate truth. That fundamental doctrine is the Trinity.

The Trinity

The doctrine of the Trinity rests on the historical evidence of the Bible. The authenticity and credibility of the Bible is a study of its own and is not a part of this essay but I have studied the evidence and arguments for and against this premise and I have accepted that it is valid in its origins and its contents. The doctrine of the Trinity is found in this source. For those who do not accept my premise about the Bible, this discussion of the Trinity is irrelevant. It was articulated in the account of the annunciation that appears in the New Testament. Christ reiterated it in his teachings during his public life. He also claimed to be the eternal Son of God.

I first arrived at a conclusion that the universe reveals evidence of intelligent design emanating from a divine or supernatural source of power, which is responsible for the creation of all that exists in the objective (and the created spiritual) world. There are two components to this power. There is firstly an intellect that conceives ideas for a creative process and secondly there is the energy to fire and maintain the system so that ideas are transformed into objective reality. From the scientific literature, we observe that energy is found operating under many forms; it makes possible the continued operations of the laws that govern the material world.

I believe that this power must be in an eternal state of existence; it has always existed and will never pass out of existence *for it is innate in its very nature or being.* It is the unchanging form of ultimate reality and gives meaning to the word "existence". Something must exist whose essential nature or essence is *to exist of its own accord.*

It is constant in all its attributes which are innate to its being. One of these attributes is that of love, for the Incarnation is all about the love of the Godhead. True love however is a virtuous interaction between two or more distinct beings (essences) and must also reside in the Godhead, not necessarily in the form that exists in our human nature but in the spiritual reality of God. Within that reality, only revealed truth from the Godhead can describe how it exists in the non-corporeal divine nature. Jesus Christ is the only being who ever claimed to be true God and true man, who manifested the loving relationship between the Father and the Son within the Godhead. He was in existence from all eternity. Christ

succinctly articulates it in the two great commandments of love.
The Father and the Son are two personalities within the unity of
the Trinity.

Holiness is another attribute of the divine nature as revealed by
Christ. It is sustained by a state of grace, a non-material component
of sanctification found only in the divine state but is distributed
from the Godhead by the Spirit of God, a third revealed distinct
element. This third personality within the Godhead seems to be
the source of energy in the power of God, the one who vivifies the
divine love and displays the holiness of God. The Spirit of God
(the third personality of the Trinity) is manifested in providing
the cosmic energy that created and sustains all material things and
beings and it is the source of grace that establishes and maintains
the holiness of the Trinity and those who seek to become the
adopted sons of the Father. This is a revealed truth articulated by
Jesus Christ who claimed to be the innate Son of the Father. " In
the beginning there was the Word (Jesus Christ) and the Word was
God."

The Holy Spirit of God is also exercised in the sacraments,
especially the sacrament of confirmation. There are seven gifts of
the Holy Spirit conferred at confirmation.

1. Wisdom.
2. Knowledge.
3. Counsel.
4. Understanding.
5. Piety.

6.   Fortitude.

7.   Awe of the Lord our God.

These gifts constitute an additional outpouring of grace on one who has already been baptised and empowers the receiver to strive for holiness. At the time of Pentecost, the Holy Spirit descended on the apostles and Our Lady, drew them into the Church established by Christ and equipped them for their mission to spread the message of their Lord and master to the whole of mankind.

Three Divine Persons

In their discussion of God and the Godhead, scholars have used the analogy of the three divine persons. In our own human existence, we have developed a concept of the *human person* to whom is attached a quality called human dignity. In the Old Testament, the first part of the Christian Bible, we find the expression that Man was created in the "image of God".

In the species of man, the "human person" is defined as a single individual entity consisting of two components, a material (corporeal) body and a spiritual soul. In his or her life on earth before death intervenes, the human person is constituted as a single entity which is subsumed under what is called its "substantial form"– a unified corporeal and a spiritual (non-corporeal) being. But Christ has indicated that the human person does not disappear at the time of death when the corporeal element disintegrates as it "returns to dust". The spiritual component does not die, so the spiritual soul alone constitutes the substantial form of the human person after death of the body until the Day of Judgment when a gloried body is resurrected and reunites with the spiritual soul.

The Trinity as the purely divine entity, as distinct from a created spiritual being (the angels), has a substantial form that does not pass through periods of change for it is an eternal unchangeable essence. Christ was unique because as a divine entity from the Godhead, He was vested with man's corporeal nature; He lived amongst us until He died on the cross. There is no mention of his corporeal remains being found in the tomb three days after his death on the cross, but his glorified body was seen on many occasions over the next 40 days.

The substantial form of the divine Godhead consists of three spiritual eternal components unified in the one eternal essence that is manifested to us as eternal love, eternal holiness and eternal power. From this eternal essence emanates everything that is in existence. For want of a better expression, these elements of the Godhead are referred to as persons even though our intellect boggles when it moves beyond the material and created spiritual world and seeks to understand the divine essence of the Godhead.

Whichever way you look at the doctrine of the Trinity, it remains a mystery, a concept that cannot be fully grasped by the human mind. Apart from some inconclusive references, it was not known in the Old Testament of the Bible nor is it a dogma of Judaism or of the Islamic religion. It is however a dogma of the Christian faith and rests upon the word of Jesus Christ who claimed to be the Son of God and one with the Father and the Holy Spirit. Then there is the voice of the Father at the time of the baptism of Jesus and later at the time of the transfiguration: "This is my beloved

Son in whom I am well pleased." At the time of the Annunciation, we hear the voice of the Archangel Gabriel who proclaims the involvement of the Trinity and finally we hear Christ who sends forth his apostles to baptise all nations in the name of the Father and of the Son and of the Holy Spirit.

Some of our difficulty is the use of the word "person". There are three divine personalities in the unity of the Trinity. The Gospels do not use the word "persons" in the context of the dogma. In our modern use of the word, we identify an individual, separate being and consequently we wonder how there can be three persons in a singular being "God". Three divine persons in the one God.

There is another way of looking at the dogma. It is universally agreed that the Godhead is a unity. In the scriptures we observe that the Infinite God does manifest himself to man in several ways. In the Old Testament, we recognise an infinite being with certain attributes – infinitely intelligent and wise, infinitely powerful, infinitely merciful, infinitely just, infinitely loving, the creator of all that exists, who creates man in his own image and who speaks of a final judgment. He lays down laws that govern all that exists and He establishes laws or commandments to govern the behaviour of those created in his own image – the species homo sapiens, mankind. But He also announces the future coming of a messiah – the Lord's anointed, the one to deliver man from the consequences of his sins.

This anointed one is conceived in the womb of a human being, to develop along the biological lines of human generation but He is penetrated by the spirit of God and is to be recognised as the Son of God as well as the son of man. Jesus of Nazareth is that being whose life from infancy through to death is narrated in the Gospels. He occasionally reveals something about himself that seems incomprehensible – during his infancy with the shepherds and the magi, at the age of twelve in the temple with the religious leaders and with his comment about his Father's business, when tempted by the devil and at the time of his baptism and transfiguration, at his meeting with the Samaritan woman and at Caesarea Philippi, at the Last Supper, at the resurrection and then his ascension, supported all the time by his miracles and prophesies.

These events all set the stage for the mystery of the Incarnation. How could a human being do all these things, unless He was God Incarnate? Or empowered by God to do so. But Jesus said that He and the Father are one.

"I am in the Father and the Father is within me", "He who has seen me has seen the Father", "Before Abraham was, I am". The mystery of the Incarnate God, the beloved Son of the Father, embraces the mystery of the two natures of Jesus Christ and his union with the Father. It imposes a tension on our usual understanding of the word "person". It gives it a meaning that is unrelated to its everyday usage and is best used with a capital P.

It seems to me that God not only wished to redeem the world from its sins through the Messiah but He also wished to communicate through the medium of a unique human *cum* divine being some knowledge about the divine nature, about the relationship between God and man and the ultimate end of man. Christ preached about the kingdom of heaven that is open to all, provided that they acknowledge the divinity of Christ and observe his two great commandments of love. To those who do so, they will attain the power to gaze upon the beatific vision, to the very essence of the Godhead and become the adopted sons of God.

9

A mixed up Catholic layman

The following paper was prepared for an after dinner speech on 5 September 2009.

Many weeks ago, I received a most unusual email from my friend, Anthony Cappello. He wanted me to write an essay for a book that he had conceived on why migrant Italians generally remain Catholics, as if there is a significant association of factors that generates an Italian *cum* Australian Catholic.

At the time, I was researching on the internet for a submission to one of those perennial committees of inquiry, probing the question of the role of believers in religion in the public square of a democratic society such as Australia.

So along came this request, asking me to write about why I, of peasant Italian stock, born and raised in Australia, within the fold of a Catholic upbringing, should still, at my advanced age, be interested in Italian culture and to be an apologist for my religious beliefs. The subject is dear to my heart and somebody may be interested in what I have to say. This is a personal story but my faltering memory may be more whimsical than calmly analytical in this selection of factors from my past experiences.

First let me sound a word of warning. The ideas that I now express were not clear to me during my evolution as a public figure.

They were not recognisable guidelines that I consciously followed as a devout Catholic, proud of my ethnic origins. But in retrospect, after many decades have passed, one can appreciate the factors that contributed to my inner convictions and the decisions that I made.

It is obvious to me now that in my earliest years, I was establishing my identity within an immigrant Italian-Australian family wherein my parents and siblings were identifiable and my comfort zone was an extended family that retained many of the cultural trappings of the Aeolian islands, north of Sicily.

I was eventually sent to the local Catholic primary school, run by the Sisters of St. Joseph. When I was in sixth grade, I was old enough to become an altar boy. That had a profound effect on me as it enhanced my understanding of the Mass and the meaning of the real Presence of God, both in the Eucharist and in the Tabernacle. The use of Latin was a bonus, for I enjoyed the lilting responses and the sense of belonging to a universal Church.

I studied Latin throughout my secondary schooling and this led to my appreciation of Church history and the spread of Christendom within the Greco-Roman culture. In particular, I was fascinated by the history of Rome and the Papal States and of the Papacy as a religious institution. So I enjoyed the study of the Latin language with its verbal declensions and its association with European history and the spread of the Christian faith. This was at a time before Italian was taught in schools and when English rapidly became our first language.

During this period, as a family we attended many functions organised by the Aeolian Society. My father became involved with

Italian chaplains who ministered to various Italian subgroups. My father was also friendly with other non-Italian priests, mostly of Irish origin but also with the Salesians who ran the annual religious festival at Rupertswood.

My deep interest in the Catholic faith received a boost in 1939 when I was awarded a prize by the Christian Brothers' College, North Melbourne. The book was *Characters of the Reformation* by Hilaire Belloc. I still have it in my possession, as I have never loaned it to anyone. It opened the way to the works of many other eminent Catholic writers of the early 20th century. But before that I had become a member of two Catholic lay movements, mainly through an interest in sport – the Young Christian Workers (YCW) and the Victorian Catholic Lawn Tennis Association (VCLTA). It was my brother Felix (Phil) who led me in this direction as he had good managerial skills and became secretary of the tennis club. He had to leave school early to help my father in the "shop" during the depression years. This meant for me that prior to going to the university, I was actively involved in local parish activities of a social nature, less intellectual than those of my older siblings, Bob and Josie, who were involved with the Campion Society and the Clitheroe Society respectively and both with the Central Catholic Library.

My decision to study medicine was influenced by several people – the headmaster of St. Kevin's College, Brother Purton, an outstanding teacher, anxious to encourage his students to gain professional qualifications, and Doctor Harry Williams, our family physician and good friend of my father. But my early days at the university were unsettling. I felt uncomfortable with few friends that I knew from my college days and confronted with subjects that were unfamiliar to me. But I attended tutorials at Newman College and became a member of the Newman Society where I established new friendships and a sense of a common Catholic heritage.

The atmosphere of the university was latently hostile to religious affiliations, especially Catholicism. I realised that I needed a crash course in apologetics and modern politics if I was going to justify my beliefs and convictions. I consulted with friendly priests at the Central Catholic Library who guided me to the works of Lunn, Knox, Belloc, Chesterton, Sheed, C.S. Lewis, Dawson, Newman and Daniel-Rops. The pre-clinical years were the most difficult of my undergraduate studies and I was glad to be accepted by St. Vincent's Hospital, under the Sisters of Charity, where I completed my course.

I now entered a phase when my Italian identity coalesced with my identity as a Catholic doctor. It was during the 1950s when a new wave of Italian immigrants settled in the inner suburbs of Melbourne. Many found their way to St. Vincent's Hospital when they became ill and needed interpreters. Previously inarticulate in the true Italian language, I acquired some ungrammatical fluency which improved when I went into private practice as a general practitioner and later as a specialist physician. My involvement with the Italian community expanded and while I did not perceive myself as a doctor dedicated to treating Italians I did enjoy conversing with them in their own language and to learn of their cultural backgrounds from the diverse regions of the Italian nation.

I have always enjoyed the practice of medicine and over the

years I made many professional friends in several hospitals – St. Vincent's, the Austin and the Royal Children's Hospital. Whilst at St. Vincent's Hospital where I was a member of staff throughout the whole of my specialist career, I joined the Guild of St. Luke. I became acquainted with other interested Catholic doctors, not only in Victoria but in other parts of Australia and New Zealand. Most of them were senior to me but all were imbued with a Catholic ethos and a knowledge of medical ethics. Outstanding among these were Drs. John & Evelyn Billings, Dr. Frank Hayden, Dr. Pat Hamilton and Dr. John Bergin of New Zealand. Dr. Peter Pearce was a significant influence as I admired his pastoral care of patients.

In the 1960s, several important events occurred. Abortion Acts were passed in England in 1967 and South Australia in 1968. Common law judgments permitting abortions were given in other states of Australia and Right to Life organisations began to emerge. In Victoria, four doctors from St. Vincent's hospital launched The Human Life Research Foundation – John Billings, Frank Hayden, Joe Santamaria and Eric Seal. Successful public meetings were held to counter the growth of the abortion lobby.

These medical practitioners became close friends of mine as did other medical practitioners around Australia and abroad. In addition, other movements were appearing in response to the Family Law Act passed in 1975, and natural family planning began a period of rapid growth as its methodology entered a new phase with advances made in our scientific knowledge of its physiological underpinnings. This in fact grew into a form of missionary activity as it became a part of the services of several Catholic hospitals in Australia and attracted the voluntary involvement of many wonderful young Catholic mothers and their spouses.

The most significant priests in my life in this period of growth were Fr. Francis Harman, a canon lawyer and bioethicist, Fr. Maurice Catarinach working with the Billings, Fr. Rebeschini, the secretary of Cardinal Knox both in Rome and Melbourne, Dr. Jordan of the Sandhurst diocese and the now Cardinal Caffarra of Bologna when he was Director of the John Paul II Institute in Rome. Another priest whom I greatly admired and often consulted was Fr. Ronald Lawler from the U.S. During this growth in my Catholic activities, at both the national and international levels, I was actively involved with many outstanding religious and lay figures from several countries. Most notable among these was the late Professor Jerome Lejeune who was moulded in the form of his compatriot Louis Pasteur.

From the 1980s to the present day, there has occurred an extraordinary development in the new field of bioethics. In Australia, this was sparked off by the establishment of the Monash Bioethics Centre under Professor Peter Singer. This grew in parallel with the new industry of modern reproductive technology. The Catholic Church struggled to meet these new challenges and the Catholic laity was often confused by the language and interpretations of many theologians who articulated conflicting responses to authoritative statements of the Vatican. A group of doctors at St. Vincent's Hospital consulted with the Mother Rectress, with the medical superintendent, Dr. W. Keane and Fr. Francis Harman. The outcome was the formation of St. Vincent's Bioethics Centre of which I was the Foundation Chairman. The

Human Life Research Foundation quietly disappeared and the new Bioethics Centre immediately had a major impact on the bioethical issues of the day. Meanwhile in Rome, Monsignor Caffarra convened an International Ethics group and I was elected a foundation board member.

By the time that I was due to retire from St. Vincent's Hospital at the end of 1988, I had accrued several positions over the years. I was president of the Australian Family Association, of the Family Council of Victoria and the Addiction Research Institute. I was also closely involved with the Billings and the development of WOOMB, the World Organisation of the Ovulation Method Billings.

My brother Bob generously offered me some office space and I joined him in the formation of the Thomas More Centre. I continued these activities for some years, commuting from the Mornington Peninsula several days a week whilst running a small hobby farm.

In this set-up, I learned how to use a computer, to browse the internet, to communicate by email and through the Skype application. I could access university libraries, download scientific papers, do literature searches, compose documents, write articles and even a book. I attended overseas meetings on the family and bioethics and maintained an interest in addiction medicine. I was appointed a member of the Pontifical Academy for Life and went to Rome on several occasions where I tried to refine a weak command of the Italian language.

I suppose that I had become an Australian "intellectual" (whatever that means) working in various fields of medicine, philosophy, theology and sociology. But my roots were in the tradition of the natural family, in the practice of the Catholic faith as it emerged from my Italian origins. But above all, I am deeply indebted to the great models of human achievement whom I met along the way. Most of them were Catholics with whom I worked within the medical profession or met in religious life. Although not all were Catholics, all shared in my devotion to the family and the elusive concept of the common good.

By the time that I was born, my parents were firmly entrenched in the Australian community and this flowed into the second generation. Five out of their six children married Australians of Anglo-Irish backgrounds so that their extended families were of mixed ethnicity and culture who shared a Catholic upbringing. One's ethnicity can be quickly submerged by intermarriage but not readily eliminated as the adopted country itself changes in its cultural formation as it embraces many of the customs of its immigrant populations.

What happens to religious belief however is much more sensitive to broader influences, particularly those of the second half of the 20th century. Some of these influences are of global proportions and the causes are many and bewilderingly complex. The Catholic Church is facing challenges of profound significance, both from within and from without and many of the challenges have been consolidated by political processes.

This brings me back to the cause of my opening reflection – should Catholics be engaged in the public square? Of course we should even as those who have no religious beliefs should also be heard. But each of us must be prepared to present the evidence and its sources for our basic premises and we need to be engaged as listeners as well as contributors using the respectful language of dialogue.

We need to be alert to the motivations of those who profess to be Catholic and who seek our votes to become our elected representatives. If they wish to use their religious affiliation to win political support, they should be recognisable Catholics in allegiance to Church teaching, not simply nominal Catholics. We are today engaged in a battle of ideologies and vested interests which infect even the scientific community as well as social and political establishments and most importantly the media in all its forms. Today our culture has been transformed into an areligious, relativistic society and if we wish to insert our values that cherish marriage, the natural family and the common good, then we must be engaged in the political debates of our times and to seek the support of our fellow citizens in a democratic society.

In the time when our parents were seeking to integrate into Australian society, their strong sense of the role of the natural family stood them in great stead and helped to sustain them during the period of the Great Depression. Their Catholicity reinforced their basic values for a just society which were strongly articulated in a series of social encyclicals issued by outstanding Roman pontiffs over the last 100 years. My Italian origins cemented my Catholic identity in a culture that was Judeo-Christian in its basic beliefs. This identity was reinforced by working in a Catholic hospital and by the numerous personalities I met in medical practice and the related field of bioethics.

It is my belief that the universality of the Catholic Church and its structures of authoritative teaching must be linked to the redemptive message of Our Lord, Jesus Christ who died for all, irrespective of their ethnic and social origins. The mission of the Church must always be true to the divine revelation (the deposit of faith) and we must seek the great models of holiness who can be found at all levels of the social life, across many religious affiliations.